JOHN GREER

MW01488462

GOING FOR GOLD

BY

JOHN GREER

GOING FOR GOLD

Ordering Information: Special discounts are available on quantity purchases by corporations, associations, and others. 1-800-732-9140.

DREAMSTARTERS

www.DreamStartersPublishing.com

Table of Contents

Chapter 1

Why Are You Getting into Real Estate?

I love real estate! I love it so much that I am deeply involved in the education of future real estate agents. At Gold Coast Schools, we educate and train thousands of individuals every year, something that we've been doing for more than 50 years. This book is a roadmap for you to use as you start your career in real estate; a career that can change your life, and help you fulfill lifelong dreams of financial security and freedom. Getting your real estate license is the first step in your career, but the information in this book is intended to help you kickstart your career.

Part of our company's mission is to positively change lives, one person at a time. For me, for example, helping people fulfill their goals and dreams is a lot of fun. We are a second generation, family run business that trains people for licensing in real estate, construction, insurance, mortgage lending, property management, and appraisal. We cater to students across the state (Florida) with online and in-person classes, in several languages, and in just about every specialty of the real estate field you can possibly think of. It's a passion that we've had for a half-century.

Now, I know why I love real estate, but before we even get started, this is a question you really have to ask yourself. What is your mindset? Your motivation? Your deep-down reason for getting into real estate? If you've done any research in the field, or know people who work in the field, you already know that it is not a pathway to instant, easy wealth. The successful real estate professional understands that hard work, long hours, and personal time and financial investment are needed to succeed in this business.

So, *why* do you want to be a real estate professional? In his best-selling book "Find Your Why", Simon Sinek explores the concept of finding what drives you.

Many people come into real estate as part of a significant shift in their lives. More often than not, they are changing their career focus from one of being an employee, with set hours, and a set schedule. Making such a change requires that you look at not just the short-term reasons that you're looking to get into real estate, but also your long-term goals and motivations.

I've seen people enter this business for all sorts of reasons; sometimes it's because something external has happened to the person. Maybe their spouse passed away, or their kids left the house. Maybe they're retired and bored. Perhaps they are seeing layoffs all around them, or they were themselves laid-off. Sometimes people get into real estate because they want a side job, or another source of income. Some of our students are very young, some in their retirement years - seriously 18 to 80, GED to PhD. Anyone can get started in this field, for any reason; we're just here to help that happen.

Even though real estate agents work under brokers, to some degree they are similar to being self-employed. It takes time to build this new business, and there WILL be bumps along the way. Just like anything, there will be ups and downs, long stretches of this new road with no income and no activity. Are you prepared for that? Financially? Emotionally? Is your family invested in this new course? Are they prepared for the ups and downs on the crazy road of starting a career in real estate?

As you ponder this, think about realistic expectations. Are you out to make $100,000 your first year? Sure, you will hear stories of people who have done it, but it's not the norm. Make sure you are setting a realistic timeline and set your priorities accordingly. How will you handle working nights and weekends, visiting strangers' homes, for example? Can you handle the constant rejection involved in this career? How about your family? Are they prepared for this type of schedule? Think about these things in advance. Talk about this new lifestyle with your partner and/or family.

You're basically starting your own business when you are starting a career as a real estate agent. As such, you - and only you - are in control of your business, and your future. People will try to steal your dreams, or put you down, so control that by staying away from negative people. Haters will always be haters. The opinions of those types of people don't really matter; they've usually not done what you're embarking on, so don't let anyone get in the way of your WHY - your dreams, your motivations, your future.

Set your long-term focus on what you need to do to achieve the things you want; to fulfill your dreams, often times beyond your wildest expectations. Tap into the energy of people who believe in you, who have traveled on this same road, and who have tasted success in this tough field. They'll encourage you - your destiny is in your hands - your dreams don't intimidate them or scare them.

This isn't a course in getting rich quick. No, this will be hard work; frustrating at times. The road to real estate success is not a smooth four-lane highway, with no traffic, no foul weather, or no hazards or blockades. Your road, like that of everyone else who has achieved real estate success is bumpy, filled with potholes and sections of washboard dirt. You'll have blind curves, unmarked driveways where people pull right out in front of you. You'll drive across stretches where it feels like you're in the middle of nowhere, and other areas where there is so much traffic, and stress, that you'll just want to give up.

But, like any good road trip, there are stretches of beauty and peace that makes the whole journey worth your while. When you can navigate the tough times, those stretches are even more beautiful and fulfilling. You quickly learn which roads and routes to avoid, and to time your travels so you don't get stuck in energy-sucking traffic. This is the nature of traveling, and it is my hope that this book, this roadmap, will help you avoid those common road trip hazards, and get the most out of your fantastic journey into the world of real estate.

Many people who start a career in real estate last less than six months. I firmly believe it is because these people didn't have a strong WHY, or weren't realistic about what is involved in achieving success in the field of real estate. They didn't talk to their family and/or significant other about the sacrifices of time that would be needed, especially in the beginning, so felt pressure, both internal and external, to quit.

It's sad, but it's okay. It takes three to 12 months to really see any results in this business, so they weren't cut out for the realities of the real estate business.

Are you? Really? Because if you are, and your family is on board, this could be one of the most rewarding road trips you'll ever take.

My WHY is different than most in the real estate business. Over the last 30 years my primary focus has been on the education side of real estate, along with personal investing in real estate. My first teaching opportunities were helping talented and creative individuals who happened to have a learning disability, prepare for and pass the exam needed to obtain their license. I loved helping them get through the exam, and get started on their careers. From those beginnings, I have directly and indirectly helped to educate hundreds of thousands of people in the real estate industry.

Through that process, I learned that some of the most successful people in the real estate business didn't pass the exam the first time around. Things didn't come easy to them, so they had to work harder than their colleagues. They had to set their goals more on the long-term than the "what should I do today" mentality. They persevered because they knew their WHY. They immediately came upon a roadblock, and didn't give up on their personal and professional journey.

Most of the WHYs that I've seen in individuals are one of the following three reasons:

1) Make a lot of money,

2) Have freedom and flexibility in their career,

3) Help people achieve their dreams.

The real estate business isn't about real estate. Really! It's not about homes, offices, land, property. It's a business that revolves around serving and helping people. I know some people, well, a lot of people who think that real estate is actually a technology business. I prefer to think of real estate as a people business that *uses* technology. It comes down to getting people to know, like and trust you and working through that process. Above all, a real estate career is about building relationships and helping people.

If you are thinking short-term, you are thinking about getting listings, meeting buyers and sellers, selling houses, land or commercial property. But, really, your goal should be building relationships where those activities can happen, and building your business by building your relationships and referrals that come out those positive relationships.

Even after all these years in the business, specifically working with and educating new real estate professionals, I still can't tell who will fizzle out in six months, who will be average, or who will be a rock star. Only time will tell. I've seen people in our classes who I never pictured doing well turn themselves into rock stars, and I've seen people who were all gung-ho, energetic and smart, fail miserably.

The people who do the best are those who understand and value the personal relationships that are developed as part of this business and who are super networkers. I really think it comes down to that WHY, and making sure that it's strong, and true, long-term and realistic. It's understanding that the importance of the service to people aspect of being a real estate professional exceeds almost anything else. Sure, you can make lots of money, but if your focus is money over relationships, you'll never truly succeed.

Not that long ago, I was attending a tradeshow, when a gentleman walked past me, and did a double take when he saw my name tag. He quickly turned back around and asked, "Are you John Greer from Gold Coast?"

I said, "I sure am. How can I help you?"

He grabbed my hand, and shook it, looked me right in the eye and said, "I just want to thank you for making me a millionaire!"

"That's great!" I replied, "How did it happen for you?"

He told me his story about coming down from New York, down on his luck, and not sure what he was going to do with his life. He came to our school, got his license, and became a rock star. He opened several offices over a five or six year time period, and ended up selling the company for more than a million dollars. "It was all because of you and your company," he said. He credited his Gold Coast instructor for helping to encourage him to chase his dreams and our school for helping him to achieve them.

Did you know that real estate related activities represent about thirty percent of our US economy? Whether or not you're getting into residential real estate, commercial real estate, appraisal or title services, mortgage lending or property insurance, all of these sub-branches of what we typically think of as the real estate business start with the purchase or sale of a home, land, or commercial property. Real estate literally makes the country's economy move. You can be a part of that momentum, and you can succeed, if you understand what's involved, and more importantly you understand your WHY.

THE "WHY?" EXERCISE

What is your WHY? Make sure it's long-term, at least three to five years out into the future. Longer, if you can. Make the description of your why as detailed as you can. Where do you live? How do you live? How are the lives of your partner and/or children? What does your day look like? Your week? Your year? Consider all these things when thinking about your WHY.

_____

_____

_____

What will be some of the challenges to fulfilling your WHY? Talk these over with your partner and/or family. How will you all support each other, or if you don't have a family, yet, what kind of support system can you create with your friends and colleagues.

_____

_____

What's your goal for your first year?

_____

_____

Your third year?

_____

_____

Your fifth year?

_____

_____

Your 10th and 20th year in the business, if applicable?

_____

_____

Your retirement?

_____

_____

Now, re-think your initial WHY statement from above. What is your WHY now?

_____

_____

"Try not to become a man of success. Rather become a man of value."

Albert Einstein

Chapter 2

Why You Need to Become an Expert

When I was 22 years old, I bought my first house. It was a mess, and needed a lot of work. I put in blood, sweat and tears for three years, and fixed it up. One day, I came home, and there was a note on the door that said, "I have a buyer for your house. Call me if you're interested."

Now, keep in mind, it wasn't listed for sale. I was perfectly happy in the home, and didn't have any immediate intention of selling any time soon. My wife had other plans. We had just had our first daughter, and she was interested in selling since she thought the house would be too small for us as we grew our family. Like a lot of guys, I needed to be prodded a bit. So, I thought, "what the heck," and I called the agent.

16

Ellen, the Realtor, answered the phone, and it was clear to me that she was serious - she really did have someone interested in my home. Within twenty-four hours we had a contract, for a sale price that was much higher than I ever thought I could sell our little house for. We closed in just a few weeks.

Had it not been for Ellen, and her diligent farming of the neighborhood, working the area, and being an expert within my specific community, this would not have happened. Since she had been working in the neighborhood for awhile, I had seen many flyers from her, so when she wrote that personal note, telling me she had a buyer, I trusted that she did. I knew she was the neighborhood expert, because I routinely got information from her every six weeks or so.

Real estate is really a simple, three-part business that sometimes gets way over-complicated. To be a successful real estate agent, you need to do just three things:

1) **Find people who want to buy, sell or rent real estate,**

2) **Convince those people that YOU are the one to help them, and**

3) **Get the transaction closed!**

Everything, and I mean EVERYTHING else in this business is connected to one of those three things. The better you can fine-tune your ability to do the above, the more successful you will be.

One of the mistakes I see new real estate agents make all the time is to try to do it all, and be it all, in the business. Now, this might be a way to learn about multiple aspects of the real estate business, selling residential, commercial, vacant land, and anything else that they can try to sell, but it's no way to become an expert. You've heard the phrase, "Jack of all trades…." Well, there's a second part to that phrase: "Jack of all trades, master of none."

Be like Ellen; she knew my neighborhood inside and out, upside and down. She could talk about the school systems, playgrounds for the kids, local shopping, where the nearest fire stations were, what the tax rate was, and what the percentage of rentals versus homes that were owned was in the community. We always suggest you start your specialization immediately.

Start to focus in one specific discipline. If it's residential real estate, start by focusing on a neighborhood or two and farm those neighborhoods extensively. Knock on doors, visit open houses get to know the people, as well as the product and find out what makes the neighborhood great.

By doing this diligently, and consistently, you will learn everything you need to know about this specific area. You can always expand later. By being in the community, building relationships, and getting to know the people, businesses, schools, and everything about that community, you will become the go-to person for the neighborhood.

Be the person to go-to when they don't need something from you. In other words, be the community expert. Be the expert on schools in the area. Be the expert on the best restaurants or stores. Be the person that people see as that expert even when they just want advice on what to do and what to see. That way, when they approach you for information, they are not seeing you as someone who wants their money - they are seeing you as a source of information. You are now a resource, versus a sales-person.

When you become known as an expert in the community, you are invariably in the right place, at the right time. This way, when someone does have a transaction that they want to participate in, they think to themselves, "Hmmm. Who do I know who knows everything about this community, or who can help me pick out the best property in the area? Jill! (or John)!" You become the natural go-to person, simply because you are visible in the community; you are a person who offers value to the community, and is not seen as a sales person, always looking for a deal.

When you've established yourself as an expert in the community, you are looked at as a responsible and giving community member. They have naturally learned to trust you, because they like you and they know you. By doing this, you've also, naturally, built valuable relationships with people

19

who, when they need someone to help them with a real estate transaction, or know someone who needs help, they will automatically think of you.

You can't achieve that by buying up billboards, putting your cards on peoples' windshields, stalking them on social media when it looks like they want to buy or sell something. Anything that precludes or interferes with building meaningful relationships is a hapless effort. Instead, offering your services and knowledge when they DON'T need you as a real estate agent, puts you in a position where referrals are almost automatic.

Likewise, if you build relationships with people when you don't need or want anything from them, you will find that this type of trust and referral stream becomes natural and consistent. These types of relationships are lasting and solid, and you will build a network of go-to people to help you when you need it, and you will be the go-to person when they need a hand.

Having a real estate license means very little. Some agents will tell you they do residential, commercial, rentals, and even a little business brokerage. To me, and to the general population, someone like that often sounds more like they are desperate to make ends meet, and not really a focused professional. Being the expert in an area means people will come to you for advice, and direction. People will run away from a real estate agent who seems desperate to get their business.

So, how do you build this kind of expertise other than the usual, "get out there and meet people?"

Real estate is naturally community based. So, in the area that you're working in, it's not just about attending every networking event, and knowing everyone. You need to really get to an understanding of what makes that community tick; what makes it work. For example, let's say you live in a smaller, gated community. There will most likely be homeowner's association meetings, so it's good to participate and understand how the board works.

Get to know the bylaws of the board, and what the restrictions of the community are, as well as the amenities. Know the community governing documents, inside and out. Get to know board members, and informal leaders in the community. Not as "I'm Mike so-and-so, and I'm a Realtor," but as someone who is sincerely interested in understanding what makes the community work, and how you can be a resource. It's important to NOT push your business cards in people's hands, but if they ask what you do, you answer that you are a real estate agent who is specializing in property available in the community. End of story.

You can expand your expertise to other gated communities in the area, or other neighborhoods similarly, but only after you have acquired the expertise in that one community, for example. People who are truly professional focus in on one area of expertise, so even as you expand, your expansion should make sense to that focus. So, for example, instead of one neighborhood, you expand your focus to several in the immediate area. Then, you expand into the go-to real estate professional for the neighborhoods attached to the local elementary school, middle and high school.

An additional way to acquire expert status is to put yourself in front of the community. For example, you can publish market statistics, or just-listed/just-sold information out there via social media, workshops, meetings, door hangers, postcards, email blasts, etc. When you do this consistently, and your name and face are visible in the community as someone who really understands not just the workings of the community, but the business of real estate in the community, you are now the go-to person in that specific area.

There may be dozens of other real estate agents in your neighborhood, but if they are only putting themselves out there as real estate agents, versus a community resource and expert, they will not be noticed, and you will. In some ways, you become a real estate celebrity, and people recognize you and your value and knowledge of and in the community.

Remember, at the beginning of this book, I mentioned that many of the individuals who complete our real estate training, and get their license, drop-out of the business within six months. They've given up and given over more of the market to you. If you stay with it, stay committed to being that expert, you will outlast and out succeed many people. Your commitment to the long-term process of being a community expert will payoff tenfold, as you become someone who people know, like and trust.

In this age of inundation with social media, a lot of misguided professionals feel that they must sell, sell, sell with every post on their Instagram or Facebook feed. In my opinion, the opposite is true. You must show commitment to your community, and your level of expertise, by giving, giving, giving. Even if you are brand new to this in your community, and you don't see yourself as the expert from day-one of jumping into this business, just start making steps in that direction, and the true expertise will come in time. Either way, members of the community will see you early on as someone who is invested and committed in the community and neighborhood that you are serving.

Several times, I've seen go-getters in class, who were very gregarious, outgoing and committed to becoming effective real estate agents in the community. They were very active on several social media platforms, being young and just out of college. The mistake they made was to keep their old page active as they built their new career; posting information and becoming a community resource. Problem is, it's hard to be seen as a community expert when there are old pictures of you passed out at a college party wearing a toga!

How you have positioned yourself on social media in the past, versus how you would like to see yourself in the future, means you might need to clean things up a bit on the social media side of your life. Chase your own hero; figure out who you want to become, or find someone who you want to model yourself after.

Sometimes to do this, you have to shed old skin, and old habits. You have to be a professional adult, whose presence on and offline is one that instills trust and confidence. You may have to take a long look in the mirror and ask if that potential client can trust you, as you are now? If not, then start moving in the direction of becoming the best real estate professional you can be.

None of this happens overnight - this is a long-term process, and one that can, literally, take a lifetime. But, it's everything that I mean when I say, "become an expert." Be that person that people know, like and trust. I've been in this business for more than thirty years, and I do feel like I'm an expert; not as a braggard, but as a valid expert. I think I reached that level about five years into a committed process to develop long-term relationships and focus.

What you'll notice is that if you keep this long-term game in mind - your long-term WHY, your long-term community knowledge and relationship building - there is a distinct shift from you selling yourself, to people selling you. In addition to what I've outlined above, here are three quick ideas to consider as you build your professional, expert image:

1) Dress the part: I'm not saying you have to wear a suit every day. But, if you're selling commercial real estate, and everyone else in town wears a suit, you should probably wear a suit. If you're selling real estate in the Florida Keys, you could be selling million dollar estates, but no one will be wearing a suit. So, dress for success, but dress the part. You don't want to show up in a Hawaiian shirt and flip-flops, but you can dress casually and professionally. Visit a professional stylist if this is something you need help with.

2) Have your vehicle reflect your clientele: If you're out to sell high-end property, driving a 15-year-old clunker is probably not going to project success. You might be better off buying a high-end car that's gently used, versus a new lower-end car. Or, consider leasing a new higher-end vehicle to save on maintenance costs, and upfront expenses. Also consider your clientele/target market. If you are selling homes in a family area, a minivan or nice SUV might be

appropriate, so you can fit more than two people in your car. If you're selling agricultural property, a pickup truck with plenty of room for passengers, might be more appropriate. Reflect your area of expertise, and to some degree, mirror your clientele. Would you buy a ranch property from someone who shows up in a two-seater convertible, dressed to the nines in a shiny suit? Would you think that person really understands agricultural properties?

3) One ad isn't going to cut it. I see it all the time; a young, or new Realtor in the area puts out a beautiful, full-color postcard, offering his or her services, but then we never hear from them again. You've just thrown away your money. Better to put out a lot of information, regularly, and consistently. Be like Ellen; we got postcards and/or door hangers from her on a regular basis.

Bonus tip - The three ingredients of successful prospecting are to put yourself in front of people consistently, systematically, and give it time to pay off.

THE "EXPERT" EXERCISE

What area/neighborhood or specific expertise do you want to develop, starting today?

_____

_____

What meetings, events, and networking opportunities exist in that area?

_____

_____

How will you develop long-term expertise; what types of information will you provide, what will you give to the community?

_____

_____

Develop a 30-day plan to start on your course of expertise:

Week 1

Week 2

Week 3

Week 4

Chapter 3

How to Choose the Right Broker for You

This is probably the most important chapter you'll read in this book; I've seen too many talented agents get trapped into working for a broker that won't support their efforts, a broker who charges excessive fees, or a broker who is not interested in developing the agent into a true professional.

Let me share a story that might hit home…

Recently, one of our students signed up to work for a broker who offered a high split - that is, the broker gave the agent 90 per cent of the commission. Sounds great, right? If the agent sells a $400,000 property listed at 6% commission, the selling office would receive $12,000. With a 90 percent split, the agent would receive $10,800. 90% sounds enticing, right?

The problem is that, time and time again, I see people choosing a broker based on this high commission split, and this agent fell into this common trap. She didn't realize that, in her contract with the broker, she agreed to pay all the marketing fees, training fees, desk rental fees, etc. Her monthly expenses became far more than her income, hundreds of dollars every month, and she left after just a few months. The broker then turned around and threatened to sue her because she had signed a year-long contract.

In my opinion, as you consider which broker you want to work with, one of the LAST things you should look at is the commission split, because there is so much more to developing a healthy and mutually fruitful broker-agent relationship. Years ago, the commission split was a simple 50/50; the agent and broker would split the commission equally. The broker would provide a ton of services like training and support, marketing and advertising, and more. Now we see brokers offering agents 70, 80, 90 and even 100 percent, and agents are still expecting that those services and support will be available. They're often in for a rude awakening.

As a caveat here, please don't think I am dissing or putting down brokers. I am not. There are a lot of phenomenal brokers in the business, and I am friends with many of them. My main point here is that YOU as the agent need to know what YOU are getting into, and find a broker that is right for YOU.

Today, many brokers have no formal agent training program. They might have video training, or someone who trains "part-time." There's no real investment in getting the real estate agent up to speed in what can be an extremely complex line of work. This short-cut training is far from full-scale, and it puts agents at a distinct disadvantage. As a result, the smart new agent will see this right away and find a broker who offers strong training, or supplement the "training" by the broker with a program like the Real Estate Workshop offered at Gold Coast (www.goldcoastschools.com).

I always suggest that new real estate agents select a broker for the right reasons, and the commission split is typically not the first reason. One way to look at how high commission splits work, with the excessive expenses on the real estate agent is this; what's better, 50% of a 6% commission, or 90% of zero? A higher commission split is not bad, but it's definitely not the most important thing to consider when deciding who to develop your real estate career with.

Especially when you're just getting started, ongoing support and training is critical. You'll need to know how to deal with that first listing when you get back to the office. What do you need to do to make sure the closing goes smoothly? After all, the client is paying you, via a commission, to coordinate things - do you know how to see a real estate transaction through, from beginning to end? Do you know how to reduce liability for problems that might occur during the transaction?

Once a real estate agent is more seasoned, THEN a higher commission split becomes more important. That's because that agent now knows their way, literally, around the block. They've experienced many transactions, they don't need as much help and support, and they know how to maximize their marketing efforts and office/desk fees. If a highly experienced agent is looking for a broker, then the commission split question is much more important, but, chances are, if you're reading this book or participating in one of our training programs, that you are not yet at the "highly experienced real estate professional" level.

There are so many other factors such as: what the broker charges in fees, size of the brokerage, marketing efforts, how leads are handled, training, support, and your comfort level with others in the office. There are probably dozens if not hundreds of brokerages in your area. This is not one size fits all. Find a brokerage that fits you, not one that fits your friends. Be sure to read an employment agreement fully before signing, and have your attorney review it if there is anything you don't fully understand.

You've most certainly heard the adage, "It's not what you know, but WHO you know." This is especially true in almost every realm of every type of business you can think of.

Finding a good fit for your broker is about finding YOUR who. Who do you feel comfortable working with? Who do you feel will support you and help you? Who do you feel will treat the agents with respect and make sure that everyone wins when a real estate deal is closed?

Do you prefer a setting that is more of a family business? Or do you think you would be more comfortable having a corporate name behind your brokerage firm? I, nor anyone else, can tell you what's better for you; this is a completely individual decision, that you might have to make a few times before you find the right fit for you, your style, the type of customers you want to serve, and the types of agents you want to work with.

At the end of the day, though, in my book, the most important question is to look to your left and to your right. In that brokerage office, if you run into a problem, or have a question, will that person on your left help you? What about that person on your right? Yes, everything else we've talked about is important, but, to me, the most important thing to consider is how it will feel when you need something, and when you have a problem, or question, or concern about a real estate transaction that you're working on.

One of my friends really felt the importance of this type of situation. She had a big deal that was very close to being turned into a real estate contract. But, she had some questions about how to proceed with the deal. Naturally, you would expect, she went to her broker and explained her concerns and questions. After she finished telling the broker the situation, he turned to her, without even blinking, and said, "Sorry, we don't have time for that. You'll have to figure it out."

She lost the deal. And she, in turn, walked away from the brokerage and from the business, discouraged and feeling broken. Why that broker didn't want to invest a little bit of time to make sure that the deal would move forward, I'll never understand. In this case, it might have resulted in an impressive commission, but the broker, inexplicably, was not invested, personally or professionally, in helping.

In an ideal world, the broker and the brokerage office will prioritize that the new agent gets and closes a deal as soon as possible. That's how it used to be; the brokerage wanted to nurture long-term relationships with the agents, and vice versa. Some brokerages are still like this, but more often than not, brokers act more like landlords and charge desk fees for someone to place their license with the brokerage firm. Those types of brokerages give out the high commission splits, because they don't care whether or not you close a deal; they'll get their "rent" no matter what, and, will make money whether or not you close any sales.

Here are some things to consider when looking for an office:

- Location of the office?
- How much the office actually works for and with the agent?
- Whether the office manager is competing with his or her agents, or is there to help new agents?
- Is there a mentoring program or team-support in the office?
- What fees are you expected to pay (marketing, transaction, errors and omissions insurance, desk fees, etc.)?

There are hundreds of real estate office models out there, and they are all different. Each one is designed by and for the individual brokerage. It's not inherently bad, for example, if a brokerage charges certain fees. However, you want to look at the trade-offs. If the broker is charging a desk fee, but they have an amazing mentoring and training program, that might be something that would be good for you. You have to weigh where you are in your career, and how much support you'll need, with what you are likely to be able to close and earn in your fledgling real estate career.

THE "BROKER" EXERCISE

Based on what you've read so far, what do you think you're looking for in a brokerage firm?

_____

_____

_____

_____

_____

Ask any friends or colleagues who are working as real estate agents what they like, and don't like, about the brokerage firm where they are currently working, or have worked in the past.

Start to think about how you prioritize the following - rate them from 1 (not important) to 5 (non-negotiable/critically important)

___ **Location**

___ **Community reputation**

___ **Area of expertise/specialty**

___ **Training/mentorship**

___ **Commission split**

___ **Fee schedule**

___ **Does Manager compete with agents**

___ **Franchise vs. independent**

___ **Ongoing support**

Chapter 4

Prepare for the Interview

As we move into this next section, and you think about what kind of broker you would like to work with, it becomes important to think about, how you can get a feel for the brokers that will inevitably approach you as you gain your real estate license. As much as they are looking for a good fit for their brokerage, and will be interviewing you, you need to interview THEM.

Let's say you make a few calls and get an interview at the brokerage where a friend works. You've got your friend's recommendation, but it's not enough to just show-up, wearing your best suit/outfit, and polishing your shoes. Interviewing is a two-way street, and the best way to conduct an effective interview that will likely get you the information you need is to prepare, in advance, of the actual meeting. From there, you need some way to sort out what you like, or don't like, about each brokerage; a scorecard of sorts.

The truth is, getting a position in a brokerage is like getting a job, and at the same time it's not. In a traditional job interview, typically the applicant is one of many, and the employer has the luxury of being very picky as to who he or she selects. When interviewing a broker, YOU have the advantage; most brokerages are anxious to get agents working in their office. As we've seen, they can make money, whether or not an agent is closing deals. So, YOU get to be the picky one.

Hopefully, by the time you walk into the brokerage office for the interview, you know what is important to you. This is why I had you go through the exercise of the previous chapter. That's where you have begun to think and consider what it is that you're looking for in a real estate brokerage firm. Just as much as the broker is interviewing you, you're interviewing the broker with those priorities in mind.

Before you go to the interview your preparation needs to include a few things:

- *Research the broker*: Ask about the broker from people who have worked with, or have done business with the broker. Look at reviews online, including reviews that former agents might have left. Prepare a list of questions if you haven't been able to find things out during your research. For example, what is their training and mentoring program?

- **Get your CV (Curriculum Vitae) ready**: A resume lists your employment, while a CV typically explains what you actually did. What is the value that you're bringing to the table? What is your education and experience in the field? Highlight any aspects of your career that will help you be successful in real estate; sales, volunteering, service to others, experience with the public, even travel.

- **Ask to attend an office meeting**: Get a feel for the morale of the office. What's the culture of the office? Are you welcome to attend the meeting? Is there a regular office meeting? Is the culture of the office good for you? Are you good for the culture of the office?

Throughout this process, don't be afraid to ask questions. Find out, for example, the process of how leads are distributed. Do you make more if you bring in other real estate agents? Does the broker or manager also act as an agent, and therefore, compete with the other agents? Do they get "first pick?" How is floor time handled? Is it voluntary? Is it assigned? Self-assigned? Ask the question, "what should I be asking that I'm not?" This specific question, along with any others that you ask, demonstrates a willingness and openness to understanding the true culture and feel of the office. These questions should be welcomed by a good broker.

I've been in the business for a long time, and I know many brokers in the area. Once in a while I hear the occasional broker complain about new agents being "cocky" and/or "arrogant," saying something like, "Well, I'm here to interview you." Of course you are, but I don't recommend an arrogant approach. You may be working with this broker on a transaction in the future, and this type of adversarial and unprofessional approach will not serve you well. Remember, this business is about building relationships, including among your fellow agents and brokers in your area.

Likewise, if you have asked these questions, and didn't like the answers, but took the offer to be an agent in the brokerage anyway, don't be upset by what the regular office procedure is. For instance, if the policy is that the listing agent gets the lead for anything that comes in during your floor time, you need to be able to accept that, and understand that that is not an unusual practice. Plus, it was disclosed to you because you asked during your interview. You did ask during your interview, didn't you?

One of the last questions you should ask is about the commission split, as I've mentioned previously. At this point, you should have a good understanding of what the broker will offer you as part of being on their team, and you can put that commission into perspective along with the other things you asked about. The commission, especially as you are just getting started, really is one of the least important aspects of your interview process. In my opinion choosing a broker who will give you the best chance to launch your successful real estate business, is the most important. Remember, commission splits will INCREASE as your production increases. You may be starting at 60%, but as your production increases, so does your share.

Don't be fooled by bells and whistles; marble floors and solid wood desks, agent vehicle allowances and pretty business cards, for example. Yes, those might be important factors for you, but it shouldn't be THE factor for making your decision. Think of what your clients might be looking for. If THEY are looking for you to be on a certain street in downtown Big City, then that can be a priority. But, if they don't care about that, neither should you.

Chances are, the broker or office manager that you're interviewing with has interviewed dozens, if not hundreds of individuals. For me, I've probably interviewed over a thousand people in my career. It takes me very little time to know whether or not I want anything to do with an interviewee. First impressions are EVERYTHING in this business. You're going to be presenting yourself to clients and customers. Present yourself to the broker or office manager in the same way. Give the broker/manager a reason to like you, especially if you are expecting them to invest time and money in you.

Choose wisely, and make sure you interview several brokers. Based on your priorities, develop a scorecard to keep track of what is most important to you - not your friends, not your relatives - YOU. No one can make a scorecard for you - we can include a sample one here, but you should really personalize it. Your priorities are your priorities, and yours alone. In the business of real estate, I truly believe there is a place for everyone, but not every brokerage is for everyone. A scorecard can help you sort out what type of brokerage is for you.

Five years in a row, we've been voted by the Sun Sentinel as one of the best places for employees to work, and in 2019 we were voted as the top medium-sized workplace in South Florida. I don't bring this up as a bragging point, but as a point of emphasis that culture is everything in a business - any business. The culture created and nurtured for the employees, agents, clients, vendors and with the community. Do your homework, and interview brokerages that have a positive, productive and nurturing culture.

At Gold Coast we offer career fairs so students can visit with as many as 25-30 brokers at a time. By attending this type of event, you will figure out very quickly what you should be asking. In my career I have interviewed a lot of people. Those that are prepared and confident are always much more interesting than those that come unprepared and know nothing about the job they are applying for or the company they are applying to work with.

Remember that you are joining forces with the broker to do business together. The broker is not hiring you as an employee. Think of your broker as your business partner. In this business you get paid for results not longevity. Try to find a broker that you don't have to graduate from or to as your career progresses.

THE "INTERVIEW" EXERCISE

Develop a preliminary "checklist" for your interview process:

List the top 5 questions you need to ask each broker or manager you interview with:

1.

2.

3.

4.

5.

Develop a "scorecard" to help keep track of the things that are important to you:

Item	Broker 1	Broker 2	Broker 3
Location of office			
Right fit for me			
Broker experience			
Fees			
Commission split			
Training/Ongoing Support			

Note: for the sake of space we have only included 6 items and 3 brokers. Make your scorecard as large or as small as you need for yourself. The items we have listed are for illustration purposes only, choose items that are important to you. You may want to interview one broker, or ten brokers. Personalize and make it your own. There is no "right number" of brokers to interview. Interview until you find the "right broker" for you.

Chapter 5

The Changing Paradigm of Training

Back in the 80s, when I got started in real estate, things were a lot different. I know, I sound like an old guy! We've already touched on some of that, including commission splits and brokerage services, like marketing, business cards, Errors and Omissions insurance, etc., but I'm also talking about how technology has transformed the business. Back in those days, a Realtor flipped through a fat book with the MLS listings that the public had no access to. Lockboxes had dials, and transactions and forms were signed in-person, versus online. So many of these changes make the real estate professional's job so much easier, but there's a downside, as always.

One of the biggest changes I've seen is the change in training, or really, lack of training offered by brokers. This is mostly because of commission splits changing from the typical 50/50 split of a few decades ago, to the agent getting a much higher share today. Since the broker is receiving a smaller share, the broker either makes it up in fees, or has to eliminate or reduce expenses. Often the training program has been the first, and/or the largest cut.

Nowadays, (in some offices, but certainly not all) the extent of training is often limited to sitting in a conference room and watching some videos. Hardly effective. This is in contrast to past practices, like the broker or manager accompanying a new agent on visits to help them with listing presentations and contracts. Mentoring is almost non-existent in most typical brokerage offices, and new agents are basically on their own, just as they are learning their new business and career. Many new agents expect training to be provided, and are surprised when they find out that there really isn't any help or support within the broker's office setting and culture.

I'm not faulting the brokers. In some ways, this is a necessary reality for them, as agents demand higher commission splits, and many experienced agents would rather have that higher commission, and pay the broker fees, to run their business their own way. It's a win-win in that case. Unfortunately, where it breaks down is for the new real estate agent. I've seen too many potentially great real estate agents leave the field because they didn't get the support or training they needed.

If you are at a brokerage that doesn't provide training, or when you select a broker whose training program is limited, I suggest you get the training you need. It can be through the local Association of Realtors, or through a school like Gold Coast. You wouldn't practice medicine without training, and I know it's not quite the same kind of career, but I think you see my point. You really do need good training and specific knowledge to practice real estate in a way that you benefit your clients, and your bottom-line.

One of my friends, Ann, started in the real estate business a few years ago. She was so excited, "I can't wait to be independent, and make good money helping people achieve their dreams!" she said to me. I was excited for her, too - it's a great business and very satisfying line of work.

Now, Ann was smart; she knew she was going to need help and support, so when she met with different brokers, she made sure to ask about their training program. One of the brokers, who was at the top of her prospect list, assured her that he offered free training and support. Ann felt like she had found the perfect fit. She already had some friends who worked with the broker, and the office had a good reputation in the community. On top of that, it was an office convenient to her home, and the commission splits were great, with 80% going to the agent.

"Training" began her first day at the brokerage. The office manager met with her, went over the contract, showed her around the office, introduced her to some of the other agents who were there, including one of her friends. "Are you ready for your training?" the manager asked.

"Yes! I can't wait to get started and jump in!"

"That's great," said the manager, "That's the kind of energy we need always appreciate. Let's go!"

They walked to the conference room, and, you guessed it, Ann was left alone to watch a few hours of "training videos."

"It's not that they weren't helpful," Ann told me later. "It's just that I thought there would be so much more help and training than there was. Looking back, I should have asked about the training program, versus asking a 'yes' or 'no,' 'Do you have a training program' type of question."

Your training should also include the technology that you are dependent on to do a great job as a Realtor. For example, do you know how to fluently use the local MLS system, the tax roll system or the specific real estate forms for your area? This is something that many brokers are not going to provide. Well, they might give you a short demonstration on how to login to the MLS system, or view the tax roll records.

But, that's about it. Remember, they are giving up more and more of their commission split to attract top talent, so this isn't a good or bad thing; it's just reality.

Later on in this book, I'll talk about the importance of investing in yourself and in your business, but I want to put a caveat on that. Please, don't get sucked into so-called "Guru" programs that cost upwards of $5,000 to $10,000. These are generally systems that are much more suitable for the seasoned, experienced agent. At this stage in your career, don't get bogged down in systems. This is not a systems business, especially when you first start. This is a relationship business, first and foremost.

Instead, spend a little money and get yourself enrolled in a good, basic real estate training program or workshop, right away. Your most important asset and tool that you have for succeeding in real estate is you and the relationships you build. The client is looking at you as a source of information; these days they can get the information or data they need about the homes, and neighborhood and schools, with a click of a button, literally.

On the contrary, the relationship that you build with your clients is so that they trust you to help them navigate the very complex world of real estate, and walk them through the closing process. For example, problems can come up during the inspection period. They will need and rely on you to help them navigate that. Or, what if their financing falls through just before the closing? They will look to you to help them - so the relationships you've built with lenders, appraisers, title companies, and home inspectors all come into play.

Don't get bogged down in coursework - there are literally hundreds of courses available from many sources including your local Association, but do get the fundamentals. After that, get to work doing revenue generating activities as soon as you can. The relationships you build will help you use those tools and basic knowledge to generate revenue and close deals that are good for all parties involved.

There are three things you need to master, as quickly as you can:

1. Your local MLS system.

2. Your local tax roll system, including folio numbers and verifying listing details like number of bedrooms, square footage, etc.

3. Forms and programs that are used by your broker and in your area. For instance: listing agreements, purchase/sale agreements, and more.

If you know these three things to get started, you'll be yards ahead of any other new real estate agent. So, if your broker doesn't offer in-depth training and navigation tips for one or more of these key skills, get that information as quickly as you can. Again, your local Association may be able to help, or a company, like Gold Coast, that offers classes and workshops can get you jump started.

If your broker doesn't have a mentor program (ask!), it's critical to learn from another real estate professional. Don't think you can learn everything you need to learn online, or only through workshops and classes. Getting a feel for the ins and outs of your area, and getting to know people, and building those ever-important relationships, is critical to your success. If you can, make a connection with another agent, and maybe even offer to do things for them, free of charge, just so you can get some experience under your belt. You never know, they may turn around and offer some help to you. That's what the relationship-based business of real estate is all about.

There are going to be days, especially early in your career, or in a new office, that you don't really have anything you HAVE to do. Do you call it a day at that point? I hope not. Instead, see if you can sit in on a closing, or help someone set up an Open House. Maybe you can shadow a listing appointment. In a typical employment situation, most of us aren't looking for more work to do when our workload is light. In real estate, it's just the opposite. When your workload is light, you MUST look for more work - we'll talk about this in the prospecting section as well. You really need to be a self-starter in this business. You are, after all, effectively self-employed. No one is going to walk by, and hand you a listing or purchase and sales contract.

In addition to getting yourself educated, building those relationships, and mastering the three key aspects of starting in real estate, I also highly recommend you get a good contact management system set up very quickly. There are many apps and programs available, and your broker might also have one available that they use for projects and communications within the office.

I use Outlook, for its simplicity, but there are many other programs, including those that have features specific to real estate contacts like Top Producer, Zoho, FreeAgent CRM, Pipedrive, Real Geeks, Masterkey, etc. Ask your colleagues and broker which ones they use and recommend. Most importantly, pick one that you think you will actually use; sometimes the programs with the most bells and whistles become overly complex to actually use on a daily basis.

I can't emphasize this enough; without basic, core skills and the ability to effectively and efficiently use technology to navigate the ins and outs of your chosen profession, you'll find yourself easily frustrated, and will want to throw your hands up in the air, and call it a day. Don't give up on this fascinating and fun career; it involves a lot of hard work to succeed in real estate. But, if you're up for the challenge, and invest the time and money needed to get a great base of knowledge and immediate experience, I think you'll find that your career in real estate might just be one of the best things you've ever done for yourself.

THE "TRAINING PLAN" EXERCISE

What training do I need?

_____

_____

_____

What training does my broker ACTUALLY provide?

_____

_____

Where are the training gaps that I AM going to need to fill?

_____

_____

_____

Where do I find the training to fill those gaps? (ex: Gold Coast, other training company, local Association, etc?)

_____

_____

_____

_____

Chapter 6

The Simple Business of Prospecting

Too often I see new real estate agents make their business way more complicated than it has to be. Yes, you have to know your stuff, and as we talked about in the previous chapter, training is key. Hopefully you've connected with a broker that is invested in your training, but if not, you've invested in your own training and education. Real estate at its core is about helping people fill THEIR needs. Beyond that, real estate can be as simple as 1, 2, 3.

1) Find people who are looking to buy, sell or lease real estate,

2) convince them to do that with you, and

3) know how to get the transaction closed!

In this chapter, I'm going to emphasize step 1 and 2, because, in my experience, step 3 just kind of falls into place once you've got 1 and 2 under your belt, and you've got a solid title company to help you. However, more than anything, that first step of finding people is where most new agents struggle. It's not enough to hang a sign over your door, and expect people to see it, and say to themselves, "Why, there's a nice sign. I think I'll give this person my money." Today, many new agents think that the mere presence of their website will open the flood gates of leads. Unfortunately, that is not the typical result.

Prospecting is at the very core of the real estate business. When you are prospecting correctly, you are building relationships with people, who will then refer people your way, and your real estate business blooms. Prospecting is about being visible, and available; not hiding in your office, waiting for someone to find you.

Not too long ago, I was having lunch with a friend who was a new life insurance agent. He was unsuccessful, and frustrated, "John, I just don't have any prospects."

I laughed, and looked at him. We were sitting in a crowded breakfast restaurant, "Joe, let me ask you something. How many of these people, in this restaurant right now, are potential clients of yours?"

He looked around, there were a few dozen people dining at the time, "I don't know, I guess all of them?"

"And," I added, "how many of them know what you do?"

He got it. "Probably none."

He was making the mistake that many real estate agents, and many new business owners make. He was acting as a secret agent; he might as well have been operating under cover at this very crowded restaurant.

"Doesn't your company have a business shirt with their name and logo on it that you could wear?" I asked.

"Well, yes, but it's $30," Joe replied.

"You've got to be kidding me, Joe. That's the best $30 you'll ever spend. When you're wearing that, everyone you meet will know EXACTLY what you do."

Unfortunately, Joe is no longer in the business. He was unable to create a pipeline of prospects large enough to sustain his business. Do you have a shirt you can wear, a nametag with your title, magnetic signs or a wrap on your car? Make sure you are using them! Do you carry around your business card? Do you have a business card - I notice a lot of younger agents aren't carrying cards. They are one of the cheapest form of advertising that you can find. I'm not saying that you should shove what you do in people's faces, but everyone you meet, and see out in the public, needs to know what you do. Do not operate like a secret agent.

Just wearing your shirt and name tag is not prospecting, though. Prospecting is serious business, and when you're getting started, it's where you NEED to spend the vast majority of your time, until you are busy with clients. To successfully prospect for potential customers, start with your own contact database. We all have them, whether they are on Instagram, Facebook, our email programs, no doubt you have hundreds, if not thousands of contacts already. This is where you start.

Step One: Find People Who Are Looking to Buy, Sell, or Lease Real Estate.

This is also a 3-step process, and a proven one at that….first:

Divide your contact list into three different lists; A, B and C

A-list people are those you know pretty well, and they probably already like you. They're generally in your inner professional circle, as well as your personal circle. These are people who will want to see you succeed, and will be glad to hear from you. Remember, you are NOT pitching a sale or deal; you are simply letting them know what you do now, and maybe asking if you can add them to a list to keep them informed of your activities, so that if they know someone, they'll think of you.

B-list people are folks who you may not know as well, but you have a decent rapport with them, and a good connection. These are folks who know you, but maybe not as well as those on your A list, or maybe you're not in as much personal contact with them.

C-list people are everybody else. And, I mean everybody else on your list. Don't filter too much when you're going through your list, unless it's someone who you absolutely have a negative relationship with. Once you've identified your A-listers and B-listers, everyone else goes on your C list.

Now, Formulate Your Plan

Figure out how much time you're going to set aside, every day, to contact each of your contacts, individually and personally. I generally recommend contacting at least 20 each day. So, if you have 1,000 contacts, that means it will take you 50 days to reach every one. If you're just getting started, either as a new agent, or in a new area or specialty, you're not going to be too busy - so, make yourself busy, and prospect for new clients and connections.

Commit to XX number of contacts each day, and if you get behind, do a few more the following days to stay on track. Always feel free to be an overachiever and do more! Make sure your contacts are in your contact management software, whatever you use, and track details of your relationship with them, when you send them notes or call them, etc. The more organized you are with this, the less time it will take, and the more personalized experience you can offer.

Finally, Take Action for Each List

A-list folks get a phone call from you. Again, you're not pushing or trying to sell. You're checking in, telling them what you're doing, and how excited you are to get started. If they think of anyone who might need your services, can they connect you? Would they be interested in getting occasional information about what's happening in the market that maybe they can share with friends? Do they know someone who would be interested?

B-list folks get a hand-written letter or note. Yes, hand-written - not an email (that's for your next list), but a quick note. Again, checking in, letting them know what you do, include your card, and let them know how you can help them out, or someone they may know.

C-list folks get an email, basically as above. Not a sell, but information about what you're up to. Personalize each one so that they know this is not a form email - It can be as simple as, "Hi Joe, It was great meeting you at the Home and Garden Show. Thought I would update you on what I'm doing these days..."

Once you have made INITIAL contact with everyone on your list, then devise a follow up plan to keep touching your list on a regular basis.

Additional Prospecting/Finding Tips

Other simple ways to prospect include partnering or assisting other agents with listings, checking out expired listings, volunteering for floor time at the broker office, and working with teams that your brokerage has. For example, some teams work specifically with buyers, others with investment or commercial properties. This is a great way to share information and learn from experienced agents who can show you more about the business. Team leaders typically have the knowledge, experience, relationships and reputation that you can learn about just by working on the team. Be sure, however, to understand how each team works regarding commission splits, lead distribution, etc. Not all teams are created equal; some of them are better than others for you, and it also depends not only on what the team can offer you, but what you can bring to the team's success.

When a new construction project or rental community opens in the area, visit the offices. Learn all you can about the development, ask questions, and ask them what kind of client they're looking for. Develop a positive relationship with these types of communities, and you may find that they refer clients to you who are interested in buying or selling, and need an agent to help them navigate the process.

Step 2: Convince Your Prospects to Do Business with You

Before people will commit to doing business with you, they have to *know you, like you and trust you*. Real estate transactions are big things; hundreds of thousands of dollars are involved in each one, and someone isn't going to want to do business with you if they don't know you, like you or trust you.

Trust is built in only one way, and that's by building meaningful relationships with your contacts. You put yourselves in front of them, and they know what you do (Step 1), and you network and help them solve problems (Step 2). You offer information, you become an expert on a particular neighborhood or specialty property, for example:

I am familiar with a real estate agent who was very new to the business, and he has a great niche that he was developed in the rural southeastern part of his state of Arizona; off-grid properties, or those that have solar and/or wind powered electricity, and independent water sources. This is a small niche, to be sure, but he is positioning himself as an expert, and more and more people are looking for these types of properties. Since he lived off-grid for more than thirty years prior to becoming a real estate agent, he can talk intelligently to potential buyers, sellers and renters of off-grid homesteads.

Step 3: Know How to Close the Transaction

This comes with education, training and, most of all, experience. There is no short-cut, but you can speed the process of acquiring this knowledge, as we've already discussed. If your broker doesn't offer this type of education or training, invest in yourself, and in your future clients, and get that education yourself either through your local Realtor Association, or through a training company like Gold Coast. Another great way to learn is by becoming friendly with title agents. They close dozens if not hundreds of transactions a year and are aware of all the pitfalls of closings. Offer to buy lunch, ask a few questions, and sit back and learn!

The potential is amazing, if you do this right!

A new real estate agent that I met at a convention recently shared his success story with me, and I'd like to share it with you to give you an idea of how what we're talking about in this chapter can play out, especially as you understand, recognize and nurture the importance of relationships and networking.

He was elated that in his first year he made over $100K. Now, that's something to brag about.

"How did you do it?" I asked.

64

"I teamed up with a group of investors who purchased foreclosures. So, I received a commission for handling all the purchases, another commission for renting, and will earn a third commission when any of their properties sell." The investment group knows him, likes him, and trusts him, so they use him exclusively for all of their transactions.

Brilliant.

Remember, most of all, building relationships and networking is not speed dating. Make your time on these activities meaningful, and you will naturally build meaningful long-term relationships. Prospect all the time. Wear your shirt!

Don't forget to share your activities list or goals with your manager, mentor, and your family. Make sure your family knows why you are doing what you are doing, is on board, and will hold you accountable. Using "Mommy or Daddy is working tonight so that we can take that trip to Disney next month" is a great way to keep family on board, but hearing "hey Mommy or Daddy, have you done your prospecting so we can go to Disney next month" might be an even better motivator!

THE "PROSPECTING" EXERCISE

Your exercise for this chapter is simple. Complete the first two steps of putting together your prospecting plan...Form your A, B and C-lists, and put together your action plan.

How many prospects will you be contacting per day?

How many days will you be prospecting using your original contact list?

Happy Prospecting!

Chapter 7

Building Your Brand

How are you going to set yourself apart from all the other real estate agents in your area? To consumers, we are a dime-a-dozen. Why should they work with you? What are you going to offer them that no one else can, or at least no one can as well as you? How would you like to be known in your field, in your area or region? Once you determine how you want to be perceived and known, the next step is to start to build that brand.

So, for this chapter, let's start there. Give this some thought. What particular areas of real estate are you interested in, and passionate about? What do you already know about? For example, your own neighborhood, or beach property, or foreclosures. Maybe you want to work with first-time homebuyers, or veterans. List your ideas here:

As you build your brand, it is critical to have EVERY single piece of marketing and advertising material share an image or clear branding. For example, as you design your logo, or tagline - every single piece of information that you put out there in the world should have that logo and tagline. Same font, same imagery, same color scheme, EVERY TIME.

If you explore the Gold Coast website and our social media accounts, you will notice a few things. First, the tagline for Gold Coast is "The Proof is in the Passing." We've used this tagline for 50 years. When people pass the exam, they'll often go on social media and use it as a hashtag. People understand it, and it's become institutionalized. People recognize it all over Florida as Gold Coast's tagline, and our role in the community.

The key thing, I think, is that a lot of our competitors have named their real estate schools after themselves, for example Jan Sharp Real Estate School. The problem with this is that if Jan isn't there to teach the class, students think they are getting a second-tier education. In the real estate business, it's a little different, but long-term, you may develop a team, or even a brokerage, and you want to avoid that kind of confusion.

So, you really need to consider branding very early in your career. As in, right now. To me, branding is what you want other people to know or say about you. This is something that you focus on as you consider how you want to brand. Your branding and target audience will change over time, but if you consider things carefully now, you can easily adapt your brand to your branding. What would you like to be known as? What would you like your brand to be?

If you start from there, it's almost like a self-fulfilling prophecy. Your focus will be on that brand and your audience. Rather, if you don't have that lined up from the get-go, you can get a little lost, and not have any idea of which direction you want to go. From there, you're letting outside influences determine your branding, and that's never a good idea. You're not controlling what people think and say about you, they're controlling you.

If you want to be known as the family friendly Realtor, for example, your audience will be families, and you'll want to get testimonials from families to put on your website and marketing materials. Likewise, if you want to be known as the ocean-front high-rise specialist, then get testimonials from those folks, and send a clear message of what you want people to say about you.

It all starts with deciding who you want to be as a Realtor, and how you want to grow from there. If you don't know where you want to go, you're never going to get there. You will get somewhere, but it may not be where you want it to be. If you start on the main road that you want to be on, you can always change lanes, but at least you'll be on the right road, going in the right direction.

First figure out your specialty - say residential. Then, think about your subspecialty - beach front properties, family homes, your neighborhood, etc. Then, think about the people who would be interested in that sub-specialty, and build your brand around those people. For example, if you are targeting families, you'll likely be working around people with other kids. What do these people do? I know when my daughters were young, we spent a lot of time at school sporting events, music and dance recitals, and at church related activities. These are likely the places you are going to find families. If you're going to brand yourself around working with retirees, you'll want to switch your focus to be around places that retirees spend their time, such as senior centers, golf courses, classes, new retirement communities, etc., and brand your activities for that audience.

Be realistic. If you're very young and you just got your license, you want to be reasonable and focus on where your sphere of influence is now, until you can grow and expand it. For example, if you think you want to target very wealthy people and sell beachfront private homes, but you yourself are living in an apartment far from the shore, you are probably not being realistic at this point in your life. Pay attention to where you want to go, but you have to acknowledge where you are, right now. You can be on a team to get into that realm, and ride someone else's credibility until you can get yourself in that door on your own.

Even as you're connecting with a broker, you will still want your own website; this website will go wherever you go, so choose your URL carefully. For example, if you start out at "Broker A," and name your website "www.joebrokerA.com" you're in trouble if you switch brokers. So, name your website/domain either after yourself, and/or include your specialty, for example, "www.joebeachproperties.com."

Same thing for your social media accounts. Make sure your branding is consistent. Your logo, your tagline, any images, fonts, colors etc. There is a lot of information available on social media marketing. Read, watch videos, and explore different ideas that will get you out there in a meaningful way that, like before, isn't pitching sales, but offering information and building relationships. Also make sure you are in compliance with all laws and rules regarding advertising. You learned this in your pre-license class, but it may vary from state to state.

Post content that's informative and interesting. Encourage people to engage with you by asking questions and looking for responses. Answer them every time and personally. Include their name in the response. For example, "Hi Dave, thanks for your comment - I think the future of green building is bright, too - it will be interesting to see how it plays out, for sure!"

Word to the wise - make sure your online image reflects who you WANT TO BE for your potential clients. Late night drinking posts might have been fun and interesting in college, but I'm pretty sure that your clients and customers may not find them endearing, and they will probably not instill a lot of confidence and trust. Get rid of them! There are services that can help you with this, as it can be tricky to get things off the internet, or at least out of most people's reach.

Another thing I see all the time is unprofessional email and twitter profile names. If you're going to put yourself out there as a professional, "sexygirl@xyzmail.com" or sexyguy@xyzmail.com is not an email address I would recommend! It might be a good time to get a professional email address, which means that your email should be attached to your domain name for your business, and not a generic email account like Gmail, Yahoo, or Hotmail. Your email should tell your potential clients what you do, for example: Amy@bestfloridarealestate.com.

Likewise, politics, especially in today's arena, can be divisive and turn-off at least 50% of your potential clientele. Engaging in social media in a way that puts your political and social views at the forefront is risky, and I recommend you keep your business, personal, and political lives separate. We often make the mistake of thinking that our friends on social media all think the same way, but reality is often quite different.

However, your clients may not fit into that profile, so if you post political things, you might turn off potential clients. You're instantly alienating 50% of your potential audience, whether you realize it or not. Since you're just getting started, you really don't want to do that. Once you grow your brand and have a base, you can be a little bit more flexible here. But, as you're starting out, keep things open, and keep politics out of your social media profile.

Ideally, set-up your business account completely separate from your personal account, and make sure you've set it up as a business page, since you'll get much more of the information you need to manage your marketing efforts, and know what is working, and what's not when it comes to engaging with your audience.

If you have Facebook, Instagram, and YouTube, as well as a website, make sure they are all integrated, and again, keep your brand and image consistent. Each online marketing platform should link to all the others, and back again. Nowadays, if your social media and online presence is lacking, so will your business prospects. Post videos of yourself showing properties, or talking about the neighborhood that you're specializing in.

For me, I don't care what people are having for dinner, or lunch. But, I do care if they have something that I'm interested in, or do something that might help me. So, your posts have to really have that audience in mind, and be interesting to them by tying in something that is going help them. If you're using technology to brand yourself, use it to bring out what you can offer. People will do business with you because they like your personality, so show it off in your online presence. Use YouTube to promote YOU, for instance.

If you have the means, consider working with a branding and marketing professional, especially as you get started. I've had some clients work with college students to help them build creative logo, images, taglines and other marketing pieces, and very affordably. If you're not great at building a website, don't! Have someone do it for you, and make sure you have a plan to maintain it. Quality is just as important as content; if your website looks unprofessional, you will not attract the quality client you are hopefully looking for. There are many services such as Upwork.com where you can post jobs for things like graphics, web design, etc. These are often a great choice for someone starting out since you can pick the price point and vendor that suits you.

Back to my shirt. The same shirt I wore when I spoke to Joe at the breakfast restaurant. I wear one like it every day. It's my brand. It's who I am when I'm out and about in the community. And, barely a day goes by when I'm at the grocery store, or a restaurant, at a gas station or picking up dry cleaning, that I don't get stopped and told, by complete strangers, "Oh, you work for Gold Coast, I was a student there." Every day that I wear this shirt, it starts conversations with people that would otherwise not have taken place.

At the beginning of your career, that's the whole point. You need to have conversations, and you need to meet and talk to as many people as you can. People need to know what you do, and how you can help them. They need to know you care, and they need to know that you're available to help when they need your services.

I've had friends who are approached, when wearing their logo shirt, with the question, "Oh, you're in real estate. How's the market?" That's a great opening, and the exact kind of opening you need! You may get that question a hundred times, but that's a hundred conversations that you may not have had without that shirt, or nametag. If you have a good smile, and can hold an interesting conversation, you've just beaten out all the people who would love to have that chat with the person standing in front of you, asking that question about the market.

My friend, Joe, at that restaurant who was acting like a secret agent, and not putting his brand out there, could have changed his frustration about a lack of prospects to an excited, "Oh my gosh, John, I don't have enough time in the day to get to all my prospects. I just had to hire an assistant."

Be Joe 2.0! Get your branding down, consistent, and be visible as a brand wherever you go in public, and online.

THE "BRANDING" EXERCISE

Do you have a current logo and/or tagline? If so, show it to others and get an HONEST opinion from them. What works about it, and what doesn't? What suggestions do they have to change or improve it?

_____

_____

_____

_____

_____

_____

If you don't have a current logo and/or tagline, do some research on who can help you put this together. Contact friends and colleagues, or find vendors, and meet with at least two potential individuals who can help you. This may be done online.

_____

_____

_____

_____

_____

_____

Do you have a business website? Instagram account? YouTube Channel? Facebook page? Twitter? Same as above. Have others give you their honest opinion. If you don't have this set-up yet, ask for referrals, and get started with someone who can help you, or find a vendor online. (Upwork.com is a great resource!)

_____

_____

_____

_____

_____

_____

_____

Chapter 8

Seven Tips to Build Income from Referrals

The secret to any sales career is getting referrals, and this is especially true when it comes to real estate transactions. Again, this is a BIG transaction for people, involving hundreds of thousands, even millions of dollars. So, when people know, like and trust you, they will trust you with that transaction. And, as you get experience, and gain a positive reputation, you will start to get referrals. Please understand that it can take years to reach the point where the majority of your business is from referral.

But, what if I told you that you can jump ahead in the line (without cheating) and start getting referrals much earlier in your career? Instead of spending hundreds, or thousands of dollars on marketing efforts to find prospects, they come to you?

In a previous chapter, I had you start with your contact list and go from there; that contact list that you have right now is your current sphere of influence. Remember, this is simply your starting point. You need to constantly be growing and shaping this sphere of influence. The sphere you start with today will not be the same in six months, in a year, or in five years.

You see this in your life, I'm sure. Your circle of friends changes as your life experiences change, as your work changes, as your location changes. The same is applicable for your real estate career, but now you must control and shape it so that your sphere of possible referrals works in your favor. IF you are continuously doing the things I recommend below, your referral sphere will grow much larger, and pay you back generously.

Tip 1: Become an Expert.

We've talked about this previously, but it bears repeating. Make sure to share your activities and testimonials on social media. Post and engage with your audience to show that you are professional and that they can trust you. People love testimonials, so make sure you have them visible so people can relate to your potential audience. Show your involvement in the community, and show yourself off as someone others would want to do business with. Position yourself as the expert and the go-to person. Make sure to reflect your audience and your community in every post that you make on social media.

Tip 2: Bring People into Your Sphere.

You invite people into your sphere by being nice to them. By being respectful. By showing them you value them. Please and thank you go a long way. Write personal notes and letters whenever you can. If you've had a great experience at a restaurant, let the manager know; now you've had a chance to talk to them in a positive light. (Make sure you're wearing your company logo shirt or nametag!) Send thank you notes and let people know how they have impacted you. This type of energy creates an infectious environment; people are drawn to, and of course, people like to do business with people they like. Be likeable and sincere. You can't fake being nice - your gratitude must be real. People will feel and notice that.

If you attend a conference or workshop, instead of trying to have a dozen shallow conversations with people, find a few people who you can have deep conversations with so you can start developing a personal relationship that may very well develop into a professional relationship.

Tip 3: Visit Often With People In Your Sphere

Reach out to someone in your sphere every day. Imagine, for instance, if you had morning coffee, lunch, and dinner with a different person in your sphere every day. That's putting yourself physically in front of 10-15 different people in your sphere EVERY week. You will quickly grow your sphere and referral base. Remember, this is not a sales meeting. It's getting to know them and building those all-important life and business relationships.

You're going to have coffee every day, and eat lunch every day. Why do it alone? Worst-case you develop deeper relationships. Best case, they might have a referral for you. Be with someone and make that connection. You have their full and undivided attention, and they have yours. Doing this gives you a reason to connect with people. Keith Ferrazzi wrote a #1 bestseller called "Never Eat Alone" to illustrate this concept.

I don't ask for business, but I ask, specifically, "What can I do to help you, and, who can I introduce you to?" Most people are not asking those types of questions, and people are very appreciative of those types of questions. I don't tend to talk about business until someone asks me what I do, and they always do. Mostly because, during the conversations, I ask them about their work, and what they're hopeful for in their future. They then, naturally, ask me what I do, or offer to help me. For example, I would tell them what I do, then say that we work on referrals, so if they know anyone who might be interested in expanding their knowledge about real estate, insurance, or construction, please let them know about what we do.

Tip 4: Organize and Follow-Up.

Make sure that you keep your contact database organized and up to date. Send regular personal emails, texts, cards, letters and make regular phone calls. When you meet someone, find something personal about them so that you can really gear any of your conversations so that you have a reason to follow up. Your follow up doesn't have to be about business; it can be about a favorite sports team, or a shared interest or history. Always treat people as if they are a current customer or a future customer. If you have a bad experience, don't burn bridges, and don't get upset with people if they are not on the same time frame as you. You never know when business or referrals from past acquaintances may come up.

Make sure you do what you say what you're going to do. If you say that you'll introduce someone to another colleague, make sure you do that. Book it right away, or make that connection by text, phone or Facebook messages immediately. If you don't, your value will immediately decrease to that person, and to anyone they might bump into who might need your services. They'll warn that person about how you didn't follow through and are not a person of your word.

Be careful not to burn bridges. I've mentioned this before, but it's so critical to meet people where they are. Maybe a deal fell through because someone got nervous, or wasn't ready to sell or buy. Acknowledge that and honor that. If you burn that bridge, that person will never come back to you. However, if you keep yourself open to doing business with them in the future, you'd be surprised with how a deal that got shut down a year before turns into an even bigger deal. Most people move or change careers 5, 6 or 7 times in their life. If you're willing, able and available for that person through just a few of those transitions, you are well ahead of your competitors.

Tip 5: Keep Track of Weddings, Birthdays, and Anniversaries.

I'm actually going to go a step further here, and advise you to take an interest in something they would not expect. Maybe it is their child's birthday or graduation date, or their favorite sport. Digging a little deeper shows that you are far more interested than the average salesperson. Find creative ways to keep in touch other than happy birthday on Facebook because the screen told you it was their birthday.

You want to make your follow-up on weddings, birthdays and anniversaries, and other events, personal and sincere. Everybody can slap up a happy birthday message on Facebook, so you're not doing anything special if you're doing what everyone else can do. Make it different. "John, I know you're a hockey fan. Are you watching the finals?" These types of messages are personal, and by asking a question, the other person will likely respond.

A few years ago, almost ten years ago, a colleague of mine sent me an autographed picture of one of my favorite sports figures for my birthday. There was a personal note, saying, "Thought you'd like this." That's the kind of thing I'm talking about. See, ten years later, I still remember that, I still remember who gave it to me, and I'm still talking about it.

Tip 6: Send Something Unique.

Not too long ago, I was at an event where they gave out cell phone chargers with a note that said, "I thought you'd get a charge out of this!" Corny? Sure! But, it gets a laugh, and people will remember you for what you did. Better yet, visit and drop something off in person.

Send something to your contact that might be interesting. Maybe it's an article or information that they might be interested in. Something different and unique from what everyone else is doing. I tend to read a lot of articles and stories online. Whenever I see something that I think someone else will be interested in, I forward the article with a short note that simply says "Not sure if you've seen this, but I thought you might be interested." These notes are responded to almost 100% of the time, and the response is almost always something along the lines of "thanks for thinking of me, no, I had not seen that." A personal note, along with that article, can really make a difference to someone, and show how much you care. Always remember, that people will do business with people they know, trust and like. By sending little notes and demonstrations of appreciation, that's relationship building in action!

When I read a good book, and like it, I'll go and buy a dozen copies of the book. I will give copies with personal notes to people. I'll let them know that I liked this book, and thought they might like it and benefit from it, too. People remember that you did that, and you also have a natural and authentic follow-up conversation. "Hey, what did you think of the book? Did you get a chance to read it? I thought of you when I was reading Chapter 7 about building a great customer base." Telling someone about a book is good. Giving them a copy brings it to a completely different level. You may be thinking "but books cost money!" You are correct, but a $12 book that leads to a $10,000 commission, or a relationship where multiple commissions are earned, is priceless.

Tip 7: Religiously Ask for Referrals and Testimonials.

Acknowledge every single referral with a phone call or note, whether that referral results in business or not. Master questions such as, "Who do you know that might be interested in…. buying? selling? renting? moving out of the area? having a baby?, getting married?, divorced?, or changing jobs?" These are all life changing events where someone might require your service. Work to develop relationships or situations where you are the natural solution to someone's problem. You want to be known as the person who's there when the need arises, and that need is very rarely there "today," as much as you would like it to be.

Likewise, once we put a system in at Gold Coast for asking for and collecting testimonials and reviews, we have received thousands. So, even if there is a bad review out there, it is outnumbered by dozens and dozens of positive reviews. You can't stop people from saying negative things about you, but you can encourage positive statements about you and what you do.

Every customer who graduates from our school gets an email where we ask for reviews and testimonials. These are so overwhelmingly positive that we post them on the internet directly. If a review is three stars or less, it comes directly to me so that we can follow-up and ask what we could have done to get a five-star review. From there, we work on any issues or problems that led to that student being less than satisfied. This is a great way to deal with reviews that you are soliciting, especially if you're nervous about them going public. You can publish your four and five star reviews directly, and then learn from your lower scores so that, eventually, like we did, you have all reviews and testimonials published online immediately.

You don't have to wait years to develop meaningful relationships and referral streams. If you spend most of your days, especially in the beginning when you really probably don't have much to do, investing in relationships as I've outlined above, you may very well surpass the referral network that another agent in the office has spent years developing. Relationship building is the number one skill set that you can develop. Referrals are a natural byproduct of those relationships.

Nurturing these relationships, and being sincere about how you care about your clients and future customers, will make you stand out. If they see you as a problem-solver, versus someone who is just out to make a deal, you'll find referrals lining up out the door. Maybe not literally, but you'd be surprised how quickly you can "age" or mature your new business by taking the time, real time, sincere time, to treat people well.

Generally speaking, referrals also are a higher quality client for you. Because their friend or colleague already trusted you, they will trust you more readily. This shortens the time it takes for someone to know, like and trust you. They already trust you, because someone they trust has demonstrated that you are trustworthy.

This also saves you time. For example, when a potential student calls Gold Coast, we ask how they heard about us. If they say from Google, we explain who we are and what we do. If, on the other hand, they say, "Oh, Mike told me about you," now we know they know what we do and who we are, so we can just jump to telling them which course might be best for them.

One word of caution. Although you would like to have a lot of business coming from referrals you will likely have to engage in some type of ad spend to generate leads. Be cautious, and make sure you are spending money in areas where you can easily track your spend, and your results. You need to make sure that you are receiving a solid ROI (return on investment).

THE "RELATIONSHIP" EXERCISE

Schedule the next two weeks on your calendar with different morning coffee and lunch meetings. Remember, this isn't a sales call. This is a relationship-building exercise. Be sincere, be yourself. Re-visit this section after you have completed 10 meetings, and answer the questions below:

What questions did you ask?

_____

_____

_____

_____

What questions did they ask you?

_____

_____

_____

_____

Is there anyone you can help? If so, who, and with what?

_____

_____

_____

Is there anyone you need to follow up with? If so, who and with what?

_____

_____

_____

Did anyone offer to introduce you to someone else? If so, who and with whom?

_____

_____

_____

What are your next steps?

_____

_____

_____

_____

Chapter 9

Budget Your Money

Do you know the number one reason people drop out of the real estate business? Chances are, you guessed it. Money - specifically the lack of money.

Real estate is an expensive business. Most of the time, the real estate agent will need to put out some of their own money, for marketing efforts, advertising and networking. Out of pocket expenses can really add up, so you have to be ready for stretches where your cash outflow exceeds you income, at least until you have developed a strong referral business, and your income is much more regular and abundant.

If your circumstances mean that you can only work part-time, you might want to consider working with a partner, or working as an assistant or as part of a team. This way you can earn money while you are learning. Talk with your broker or manager to determine a realistic budget.

There are two aspects to budgeting that are important to consider. First there is the process of establishing the budget. This makes you think about things that you might not have thought about otherwise. The thought process is almost as important, and sometimes more important than the actual budget document.

The second part is that the actual budget document helps you track where your money is going. A lot of people don't really realize where their money is actually going. So, for example, I suggested having coffee lunch with someone every day. Well, if you're spending $30 or $40 dollars a day on lunch and coffee, that's going to add up fairly quickly. Are you spending too much on that? Is it something you can economize? By tracking what you're spending, you can then value and prioritize things to work in your favor versus working against you.

Utilize the services of an accounting professional, especially if tracking your finances is not your strong suit. They can provide weekly, monthly and quarterly reports on how you're doing. They can also make the process of filing your taxes (more on that later) easier. So, don't just throw your receipts in a shoe box, make sure you organize them and track them so that your accountant can focus on things that will help you learn how to manage your money best. The small amount of money needed to hire a good accountant can save you tens of thousands of dollars, or more, over your career.

When you're first getting started, it's best not to spend money on anything that doesn't provide a direct return. You'll always have to come up with money for things like Realtor association dues, and any monthly fees your broker charges. But, don't start spending any of your other money on something that won't result in possible income. Other than training and necessary tools, spend money on things that will drive revenue and results. Don't be tricked into shiny objects.

Your goal is to be profitable and to last a long time in this business. At the beginning, especially, it's almost like the game of Survivor - especially the "outlast" part. You'll likely be working as an independent contractor instead of as an employee, so make sure you're setting aside money for taxes and withholdings. I highly recommend that you work with an accounting professional to make sure you're doing this, and that you're keeping excellent track of tax deductible expenses. I've seen far too many people end up at the end of the year with a huge tax bill that they weren't expecting.

I knew someone who didn't set aside money for his taxes, so decided not to file a tax return. The next year, he did the same thing, even though he certainly should have known better that second year. Well, the third year, he got tagged for an audit, and ended up owing something like $300,000 in taxes and penalties. This could turn into a criminal offense of tax evasion, which you certainly don't want to have on your plate. That will hurt your brand for the rest of your life.

Most everyone will recommend that you need 3-6 months of money in your savings when you get started in real estate. That's reasonable advice, but remember, everyone is different. No one knows your exact situation like you do. There are plenty of agent success stories where agents start with little money, but budget well, and work hard to get started quickly. There are also stories of well capitalized agents that never do anything in the business. Work with your broker or manager, and set reasonable expectations.

You can avoid the trap that many beginning real estate agents fall into - if you take the time to put together a reasonable budget, and most importantly track how you're doing within that budget, This will help you can get through your first months comfortably. Below is a sample budget that you can modify, and there are also budgeting programs specific for real estate agents. These can be great tools as you start on your way to true financial success and independence as a real estate agent.

As you start in your career, focus on activities that will get you in front of people, and known in the community, that don't involve spending on advertising and marketing. After you've truly exhausted that, and the people in your sphere of influence, then you can dabble your hard-earned money in ways to expand your exposure. Work with your broker to see what they might include in their package. For example, maybe they provide a certain number of door hangers a month, or postcards. Attending open houses and broker opens is free to do, without spending a dime on advertising.

THE "BUDGET" EXERCISE

Talk to your broker, or other experienced real estate agents in your office, to determine a good starting point for some of your expected expenses, and come up with a three-month budget. Track it here, and adjust when you build a more educated budget for the next three months:

Item	Month 1 Budget	Month 1 Actual	Month 2 Budget	Month 2 Actual	Month 3 Budget	Month 3 Actual
Buyer Leads						
Seller Leads						
Client gifts						
Coffees and Lunches						
Social Media						
Open Houses						

Website/SEO						
Photography						
Print Marketing						
Client Advertising						
Content Creation						
Dues and Membership						
Vehicle						
Other						
Total:						

Chapter 10

Time Management

I was recently with a group of CEO's, and one in particular was not having a great day.

Now, this is a guy who is a CEO of a highly successful business. He makes a lot of money, and from the outside he would seem to have it all. A nice car (well, several), a beautiful home, and a great family. He is living what most people would describe as the American Dream., coming from a traditional middle-class family background to financial wealth and stability.

But Ed seemed eminently sad to me. He was burned out. "I haven't had a day-off in 17 years…" he explained to the group. The group quizzed him about holidays, weekends, kid's events, etc. He told us that he had never attended one of his children's events.

Now, this makes ME sad. Money is important - it's true that it can't buy happiness, clearly, but it can make life easier. But, making money should not come at the expense of spending time with your family, your own health, and the well-being of yourself and those who are closest to you.

So, before you go any further in this chapter, please go back and review the chapter at the beginning of the book where we discuss your WHY. Why are you getting into real estate? Is it just to make money, or is to make your life, and the life of those you love better?

Review your WHY and write it down here:

In an employment situation where you work for a company, you trade time for dollars. If you are working in retail, for instance, you may be trading your time for $10 per hour. As a plumber you may trade your time for $80 an hour, and as an attorney you may trade your time for several hundred dollars per hour. You are still trading time for money.

In real estate you are typically compensated with a commission or a percentage of the overall amount of business you do. Your compensation is tied to your production, not your time. Therefore, it makes sense to spend 80 percent of your time on the 20 percent of activities that actually make you money.

Look at the three circles below:

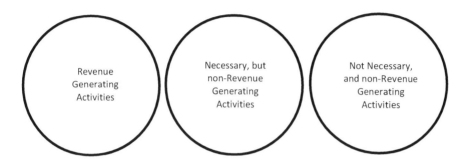

In the first circle, write down the things you do that generate revenue. In the second circle are things you have to do, but don't generate revenue. Finally, in the third circle are things you don't have to do that don't generate revenue.

For example, in circle 1 would be prospecting, and conducting open houses. In circle 2 we would find things like grocery shopping, washing your car, and cleaning your house. They are necessary, but don't make you any money. In the third circle we've got things like surfing the internet, watching tv, talking at the water cooler.

For the next week or month, record all activities in the three circles. Your goal is to eliminate (or greatly reduce) items in circle 3, delegate (eventually) things in circle 2, and focus as much of your time as possible on circle 1. As you eliminate wasted time from circle 3, add something to circle 1. For example, you're spending an hour less watching tv every day, what are you going to do to generate revenue during that extra productive hour?

In an ideal world, you are spending 100 per cent of your time in activities related to circle 1. Now, that's never going to happen, but you want to shoot for as much as possible. Delegate what you can from circle 2, and limit doing things that don't serve you (circle 3).

Don't forget to schedule in free-time. No, it doesn't generate revenue, you don't "have to do it," but it will, in the long term, allow you to generate wealth and well-being. Make sure that it gets scheduled and prioritized. The three circles have to do with business time, so in your free-time, non-business time, you need to take care of those priorities. Again, remember your WHY.

I have seen agents who are not having success, and when they do this exercise, they find out they are literally spending 4 to 6 hours a day on social media, goofing around. That might be why they're not succeeding!

Achieving greater results means changing habits. For every negative or time wasting habit you eliminate, choose to replace it with a productive or income generating habit. The only way this works is to keep notes, a diary, a journal, a log…whatever you want to call it. Be sure to schedule free time. Don't be like Ed at the beginning of this chapter.

Listen, there are plenty of books and articles on time management. If you have not seen Steven Covey's demonstration of time management using big rocks, look it up on YouTube, it is eye opening. Take care of, and schedule your largest and most important items first, especially those activities that will generate income either directly or indirectly. Fill the rest of your time in with less important items.

Things like prospecting should be huge items for you and should be the first thing to go on your calendar. That said, don't forget to schedule free time and family time. Free time helps to rejuvenate and keeps you energized. One of the first rocks you should place in your time management bucket, per Steven Covey's demonstration, is you and your family.

Here are some additional tips on how to best manage your time:

- Utilize Technology: A good CRM program can automate many of your most mundane activities. For example, by tracking leads and special events, like anniversaries, birthdays, workshops, and open houses, you can save a lot of time by having the CRM program help you organize and navigate this type of relationship building. There are several CRM programs specific to real estate work. I can't recommend any particular programs, but talk to your colleagues, and find out what they use. Doing four hours of research and set-up will save you that many hours in your first week using the program. I also recommend that you use only one calendar. I've seen some people try to use one calendar for work and another for personal items, which invariably ends up resulting in a mess.

- Delegate: Much of your time, too much of your time as a real estate agent is often spent on mundane tasks like listing entries, posting social media content, finding leads and contact information, appointment scheduling and more. There are virtual assistant services available, including those who speak multiple languages, who can make phone calls, enter data, and post for you.

- Hire an Inbound Sales Associate: If you want to nurture cold call leads, you might want to hire an ISA; they can make sure your leads are high quality and the cream of the crop. Depending on your state, these individuals might need to be licensed, so check with your broker and state law first.

- Spend money on lead generation: It's true, I apologize, but it does take money to make money. The more money that you spend wisely on lead generation, the more leads you will get, and the more deals you will close. Here's how much this will work in your favor; more than 70% of sellers only interviewed one agent. If you are that agent, because you thoughtfully and respectfully farmed a lead, chances are you will get that deal. Then, if you do a good job, and nurture referrals, you will get two, three or more leads from that first lead.

- Block off time: Instead of calling people to generate referrals all throughout the day, block off an hour or two, say from 10:00 a.m. to 11:30 a.m. to make those calls. Instead of posting to your social media accounts all day, do so first thing in the morning at 8:00-8:30, for example. Don't be a slave to the time block, because things will come up, but a structure like this will help you focus your efforts, and get more things done in less time.

- Take a break: It's been demonstrated that taking little breaks, once an hour, makes you much more productive. Get up, walk around the block, chat with colleagues about something besides real estate (well, not while they're working!), or just take a five minute meditation. The important thing is to change your position, get up and move around, stretch your neck and back, have a glass of water, and give your body and mind a little rest. It takes time to make time.

THE "TIME TRACKER/DELEGATION CANDIDATE" EXERCISE

Here is a sample template of a Time Management Log. Use this every day for at least the next 30 days (make extra copies as needed) and analyze your time management skills. (There are also convenient apps that you can use - just do whatever is easier for you, and uses the least amount of time to track and analyze!). Using this tool you will identify where you are spending your time, and also, by identifying items as being in circle 1, 2, or 3, you will quickly identify areas that can be reduced, delegated, or eliminated.

Date:

Daily Goal 1:

Daily Goal 2:

Start Time	End Time	Activity	Circle 1, 2 or 3?	Comments, Results, Energy Level

Chapter 11

Learn to Invest in Yourself

Investing in yourself is about taking the time to give yourself the resources and education that you need in order to succeed in your work, and in life. It's not just enough to get a piece of paper or a license, and call yourself "done." Once you think you know it all, or act like you do, in my book you are done. The importance of investing time and yes, money, into tools, education and investing in your career through personal dedication and perseverance is priceless.

"Life is a journey, not a destination," said poet Ralph Waldo Emerson. I think this can be adapted even further to, "Education is a journey, not a destination." When we think that we are done learning, then we are done growing and expanding our horizons, knowledge, perspective and abilities.

Education, in this case, isn't just about formal education, either. It can mean what you learn on the job, what you learn about yourself, and how you utilize tools and trade habits to learn and grow in your career in real estate.

I was in my early 20s when I graduated with a Bachelor's degree in business. Not unusual, right? Most people who get their college degrees do so in their early 20s. But, at that time I was serving full-time in the Air Force. I had attended night school, primarily out of necessity. I knew that even though my education in the Air Force was phenomenal, certain skills wouldn't necessarily translate, so I decided to go for it, and get a Bachelor's degree to help pursue my business and professional goals.

Later, I jumped into the real estate education business, and loved it. But, I realized that I had a gap in my knowledge and understanding of how best to work with adult learners. As you can imagine, there's a big difference in how to teach children versus how to teach adults, and even though I was successful in my job, I wanted to master, literally, how to do this, so in my 30s, I went back to school to get a Master's in Adult Education.

As my career expanded, along with the services that my company was offering, I jumped back into school, in my 40s, and earned a Doctorate in Educational Leadership and Management. I've found that this level of education not only gives me a credibility that others in my field may not have, more importantly it gave me knowledge and perspective that I could not have gained any other way. In addition to my experience in business, the formal education I received has fostered a lifelong love of learning. These experiences also helped me expand my network by building relationships with peers across the country.

So, the short story here is that I encourage you to be a lifelong learner. Often real estate agents focus only on networking and educating themselves within the real estate community. In my opinion this is a mistake. With today's technology, learning does not have to be formal. Watching YouTube videos of other successful agents doing listing presentations, overcoming objections, etc., are all still forms of learning. I feel that your lifelong education and training should focus on three areas:

1) *Job Related.* Here, the importance of attending association and industry conferences and classes is a good place to start, and can't be overemphasized. I encourage you when you are starting out to focus on local events and conferences. Get to know people, and make connections in your area of the market. In addition to what you learn, you will meet other real estate professionals that you can potentially partner with and expand your servicing market.

As you build and expand your local reputation and referral network, consider national training opportunities, but make sure you focus on the local/regional trainings before you go to a national training conference. Here, the saying, "Think Small" is a good thing!

Make sure you know the basics of being a Realtor; your MLS system, tax rolls, forms, etc. Expand your professional development on how to be a Realtor, and how to be the best real estate agent that you can.

2) *Training on running a business.* This is a problem in most fields. New sales associates, or doctors, or auto mechanics who are venturing out in the business realm know their craft, but they don't know how to run a business. The most talented chiropractor in the state will fail if he or she doesn't know how to run and grow their business. The most amazing chef will crash and burn if they don't know how to run and grow their restaurant. I've seen this countless times, including in the real estate business.

I've also seen real estate professionals who started in my business the same time as I did and who are still doing the same thing, the same way. In some cases, they've spent a lot of time attending Realtor and industry-type events, serving on committees, and even joining their state's regulatory board. Many of them enjoy enviable reputations and are well known in the real estate community, and although they might appear successful, they are trapped at the same point or worse off than they were before.

In the meantime, my business has grown six to seven times in the same time period. I believe one of the keys to my success has been attending training with other CEOs in unrelated businesses. Not only do you end up getting referrals from many other sources, your network builds very wide and very deep.

Do you know how to manage employees? Company financing? How to invest as a corporation, and how to organize your business, or general trends in the economy?

3) *Obtain training on yourself.* I'm no self-help guru, but I can tell you that the value of self-improvement, self-help, or whatever you want to call it, is incredibly important. I believe that, in over 30 years in business, learning how to be a better person, how to be a go-getter and self-starter, and investing in my own education has helped me to better serve those around me. You absolutely need to continue to learn, grow, and get better. In 30 years, I have spent hundreds of thousands of dollars on training and education. It is by far the most profitable investment I have ever made.

I firmly believe that if I had stopped with my Bachelors degree and real estate pre-license course, I would not be anywhere near as successful today. I might be successful and comfortable, but I don't think that I would be as happy in my career as I am. Nor would I be as financially successful. There are many great thought leaders that you've probably heard of, and I recommend that you subscribe to some of their programs or podcasts to hear their career growing philosophies. Not everyone will be right for you, and be wary of investing too much money, too early in your career, but many real estate professionals I know have benefited greatly from this type of self-improvement education.

By investing in your education, long term, your knowledge, expertise and personal and professional tool kit will have you better off than most of your competition. Start now by investing in a proper education and training program to get a good solid foundation for your career in real estate. It does take money to make money, as we've mentioned. It really is true. Spend as much money on your education as you can afford, and put together a plan.

Writing down your goals in this book is only half of the first step. To make these goals come to fruition, they have to be real, and not afterthoughts. So, either tear out this page, make a copy of the goals, or rewrite them in another format, and put them somewhere else. This new place has to be visible, every day, so that you can see where you are going, and remind yourself, every day, what goals you have for your life, education, and self-improvement. Share your goals with your family and your broker. They can help you with accountability, which will be key in achieving your goals.

Additional Tips on Investing in Yourself

As I mentioned previously, investing in yourself isn't just about spending money on acquiring an education. It is also about investing the time and dedication needed to become an exceptional real estate professional. It means taking your job seriously. It includes taking your role in the real estate field seriously. It means understanding your time and energy at the brokerage office as a necessary activity that will further both the goals of the brokerage but also your own personal and professional goals.

This includes activities like holding yourself accountable to your partner, your children, your broker, the brokerage office manager and your real estate clients and colleagues. Of course, ultimately you're accountable for your own words, actions and deeds. I've heard coaches say, "Your realm of control ends at the tip of your nose." In other words, there isn't too much in this world that we have true control of. But, we do have control of what we do, say and think.

Oftentimes, people are slaves to their emotions. They think that whatever emotion pops up is the one that they have to deal with, and they can't really control that. But, I strongly disagree. You control your feelings by controlling your thoughts. Regardless of what you might initially think, you have 100% control over what you're thinking.

Find yourself thinking something negative and draining? Think of something else. Find yourself reflecting on a particularly upsetting moment of the day, and now you're getting upset about it? Think of something else, or re-focus your thinking to think of solutions versus barriers. Don't believe me? Read Jesse Itzler's book, "Living with a Seal." He might be able to convince you.

One of the ways to take control of what you think and do is to keep an activity log, like we gave you at the end of the previous chapter. This is a simple journal that you can record either in a written paper and pen form, or there are simple apps that can be used. Either way, developing the habit of jotting down your activities for the next 30 days is a great way to focus yourself, hold yourself accountable, and evaluate your activities at the end of the month to check-in with yourself. Are you on track? Where are you getting distracted? What are you doing well? Where do you need to improve? What can you delegate?

As with your budget, your prospecting plan, and your time management plan, make sure these are in writing, visible, shared with your significant other, and with your broker, manager or accountability partner. Don't lie to yourself as you are recording what you are doing. If you ask a coach, broker, or accountability partner for help in growing, one of the first things they will ask for is your activity log. If you've lied on the log, you're only hurting yourself. Solutions to many problems lie in your activity log. You only respect what you inspect, and if you want to succeed, you must have a plan and follow it.

Remember that a successful agent is one that gets what he or she wants out of the business. Define what success means to you. This definition may change as your career progresses.

THE "EDUCATION" EXERCISE

Where do you want to be five years from now in your career?

_____

_____

_____

How about at the end of your first year?

_____

_____

_____

What educational programs or training might help you get there? Start building a plan today? Jot down some ideas…

_____

_____

_____

Of the above, which do you think are the most important items on your plan? Prioritize them, and rate them with 1 being the most important. Then, add dates for when you would like to see them achieved.

Rank/Rating	Area I need to grow and educate myself on	Date I will achieve this

Chapter 12

Next Steps on the Road to Success

The primary focus of this book is to give you tools and resources to become a highly successful and respected real estate agent and professional in your community. So, we've given you some key tips on how to jump start your real estate career, starting with learning how to manage your time, invest in your education, and mine for prospects. This core knowledge is so critical, that I always start here. If you'll remember from the very beginning chapters, it's critical that you gain the knowledge, get the connections, and close deals. When you can do that on a consistent basis, word will get out about you, and you will then have built a fantastic referral business.

But, what happens when things don't look the way you thought they would. Let's say you set a first-year goal of making $70,000, but you only reached $60,000? Is that a good thing? I mean, you reached a great income for the first year, but you fell short of your goal. Do you kick yourself for failing, or do you celebrate how far you got in your first year? I would choose the celebration!

On the other hand, what if you're setting your goals too low? For example, let's say you target yourself to make $40,000 your first year in real estate. In many markets, that target is easily achievable. So, is it too low? If you can reach it without really trying very hard, but you really need $100,000 to live comfortably, maybe you're setting your sights too low. If you're hitting all your goals, they probably are too low. So, you need to adjust. Celebrate your successes, and learn from your misses. You can also avoid burnout this way. Make your goals attainable, but challenge yourself.

This brings up the question of when you start your career, and things are off to a good start. You're meeting most of your goals, you've built a great referral network, you are closing deals and making a living as a real estate agent. You love your work, you enjoy your colleagues (or, at least most of them), and you're feeling pretty comfortable that you know what you're doing. Maybe you reach a point where things almost seem to be on auto pilot. If this is you, it might be time to consider expanding your career (More on that later.)

But, let's say things are still difficult. You're working 60, 70 or 80 hours a week. Sure, you're closing deals, and making a decent living. But, are you getting down time for yourself or family and friends? Are you working so hard, that you are missing out on the true pleasures of life? Remember my friend, Ed, who had not had a day off in 17 years, and who missed out on his children growing up? This means that your next step might be to reprioritize your time.

Think about the three circles we covered in the chapter on time management. In the first circle, you wrote down the things you do that generate revenue, directly or indirectly. In the second circle were things you have to do, but don't generally generate revenue. Finally, in the third circle were things you don't have to do that don't generate revenue, either directly or indirectly.

If you're struggling, or you know there is room for a lot of improvement in how you are doing as a real estate agent, it might be a good idea to revisit those circles, and how you're doing. Hopefully you've eliminated a lot of the activities in circle three which were things you were doing that were not producing revenue. Unfortunately, you've probably still got a lot in circle two. These are things that have to get done, and we talked a little about farming some of these tasks out, and delegating others to either online or virtual assistants, or perhaps someone that you hire to help you focus on things in the first circle – making money.

If you still have too many things in the second circle, I highly recommend you consider hiring an assistant to take care of these tasks, so that you can continue to grow and improve on your revenue generating activities. Remember, I'm pretty sure you got into this business because you wanted to make money selling houses, probably not because you wanted to spend hours every week researching expired listings, or searching sales by zip code. These are things you can easily delegate.

Expanding Your Horizons

What do all real estate brokers have in common? At one time, they were just like you. They were bright-eyed, and bushy tailed real estate agents who didn't know, necessarily, what they were doing. They had to ask questions, they had to learn the hard way. They made mistakes, and lost deals. They still do. But, they all started out as real estate licensees.

If you think you have what it takes, after a few years in the real estate business, you might want to expand your horizons and explore other pathways in the real estate industry. Many real estate agents, for example, find out that although they like the field of real estate, they're not necessarily cut out to be a residential real estate agent. The good news is, there's much more to explore.

Most of us, when we think about the real estate business, and the money that can be made in the field, we think of the residential agent. However, that's just the tip of the iceberg. Yes, a real estate agent is a key element in many successful real estate transactions, but certainly not the only element in the transaction when it comes to the variety of real estate professionals that are involved in each deal.

For instance, there are appraisers, home inspectors, mortgage brokers and loan officers, the real estate title insurance company, surveyors, investors and more. Of course, there is also the real estate broker.

A logical next step, if you find that you love this type of career is to consider becoming a broker, or real estate office manager. Maybe, someday, you would even want to own your own brokerage company. Either way, as I mentioned in the chapter on investing in yourself, I recommend you come back to school and get your broker license. You might also want to get a mortgage license or CAM/Property Manager license to open up opportunities for other areas and higher income potential.

My point here, I guess, is to keep an open mind about your future. Keep growing and setting your sights higher. This is a big change from what I told you at the beginning of the book. I recommended you start small, and stay small, until you got a good feel for what you were doing, and you could expand from there. As your expertise grows, however, it's a good idea to branch out and develop other income streams.

This is a great personal finance strategy, as well. If you have a couple of ways to make income, but in a related field, so that you're not too distracted with other types of activities, you won't have to worry if one income stream falls through. For example, if you are involved in real estate sales and you also have real estate investments, you may have more income stability. If you are a residential agent who owns investments and also manages property for others, you may have even more stability.

With that said, don't spread yourself so thin that you're losing out on developing your expertise and market. It's a fine line, and an easy one to inadvertently cross. For example, switching from commercial to residential real estate after only practicing as a residential real estate agent for one year could be a dangerous move. You haven't developed true expertise and knowledge. It may seem that you're just hopping from one field to another. Be deliberate, cautious and smart about how you expand your services. Go slow.

A couple of stories will illustrate these points, I think. First, meet Jerry. He's new in real estate, recently joining an esteemed brokerage in his area. This is a complete career change for Jerry, since previously he was involved in the oil rig business, and worked all over the country on rigs. He would spend three, four or six months away from his young wife and two children. Jerry wasn't happy, so he started looking at alternative ways to support himself and his family.

One of his friends turned him onto a nutrition-supplement MLM (multi-level marketing) company. Though Jerry had some success, of course it came slow, and it wasn't enough. Another friend invited him to become a real estate agent for his firm, and Jerry thought that would be a great option. After he got his license, he jumped in and did a wonderful job. He found prospects, found people their dream homes, and quickly established himself as a productive agent in his local real estate market area.

However, Jerry still dabbles in the supplement company, and not long ago, he took a short-term oil rig contract job to generate some quick cash. As a result, for those months, his real estate business dwindled, and he lost focus. He struggled to get back in the groove, but by the time he came home from the oil rig job, the prime sales window for the year had passed.

Jerry had not focused on his real estate career, and what was once a promising outlook for him and his family got diluted by trying to do too much, and not being able to say no. Hopefully he will regain his focus and make better decisions the next time.

On the other hand, consider the story of Don. He's another go getter, in a different field. Don is a renowned chef in the southeastern United States. At a young age he was nominated, and eventually won a very prestigious award; probably the most prestigious award a chef can attain.

Don's restaurant was a screaming success, demonstrating a fusion of traditional and new takes on soulful Southern cooking, featuring local produce and locally sourced proteins, include area raised gulf shrimp, grass-fed beef, and free-range pork. He was an "overnight" success after working for more than a dozen years in the business, starting out as a busboy, and working his way up to line-cook, sous chef, and then executive chef.

It was an exciting time; Don was featured in prominent cooking magazines, and in television spots. But, he got greedy. Within the first year of him winning the award, Don opened three new restaurants, spread out over hundreds of miles. Each restaurant, though southern-food based, had a different feel and personality, including different locally sourced ingredients. They all became a huge success. Don traveled between the four locations, every day, sometimes visiting all four in one day. So, there was a price to pay.

Don's body started to protest. He noticed a trembling in his right hand. His right eye became blurry. He was struggling with keeping the pace. He self-medicated with alcohol, and eventually had to shut down all of his restaurants and start his life over. He had done too much. He was now done.

So, it becomes critical to find a balance between working hard toward your goals, and working too hard. Again, this goes back to your WHY. Is your WHY to work so hard that your health starts failing? Or, is your WHY to make a better life for you and your loved ones. Are you on track for that type of life? Think ahead, and make sure you have several options and directions that you can go in, while at the same time maintain your focus.

For example, what if Don had just opened one additional restaurant? Maybe a more casual version of the gourmet restaurant that he had opened, or a similar restaurant in a neighboring town. Maybe this diversity would have protected him from an economic downturn, and at the same time, not stretched him so thin that he lost his health.

So, as your expertise has grown, maybe now you can branch out into other areas to develop other income streams. Maybe now is the time to dig deeper into community involvement, and charitable organizations to expand your reach. Start thinking about where you want to go, after you've reached a level of expertise that can't be argued. Where do you go from here?

THE "INCOME EXPANSION" EXERCISE

Write down some ideas of possible other real estate income that you might, at one point, consider adding to your career:

Meet with a real estate professional, in the next thirty days, in each of the following areas. Ask them what they like, and don't like about their chosen profession. Write some quick notes about what you learned:

Appraiser

Title Agent

Mortgage Broker

JOHN GREER

Insurance Agent

Real Estate Investor

Residential Agent (if you are in Commercial real estate, or vice-versa)

Chapter 13

Building Long-Term Wealth in Real Estate

Ever since the first day of me teaching pre-license real estate classes 30 years ago, I have always emphasized that true wealth in real estate RARELY comes from selling homes for others. Sure, you can make good money, in fact great money, by selling homes for others. But, in my experience, from that first day to now, thirty years later, I see that when it comes to true financial independence and wealth, the best strategy is to branch out from just selling homes for others.

In my opinion, the true wealth in real estate is created through ownership.   It usually involves owning real estate, or owning and building a real estate based business that is scalable and saleable.

Let's start with the idea of investing in real estate. If you don't already own a house, put this at the top of your list of things to do. Not only is a home a great way to save for retirement, it can also be a source of ongoing funds if you choose to later rent it out, or sell it. If you're up for the project, buy a fixer upper, live in it, fix it up as you go, and sell it. Continue this cycle, gaining capital and principal every time. You'll find this is a great way to get started in your own practice of real estate investing.

In the real estate business, one of the great advantages that you have is access to properties or deals, often before they are known to the general public. These are some of your best opportunities, as you can take advantage of the availability of great real estate investment properties, and jump on wonderful homes that can make you some real money.

I purchased my first house when I was twenty-two years old. The opportunity came from a mortgage broker friend telling me about someone who was about to lose their house to foreclosure, and couldn't qualify to refinance or restructure their loan. This was a great way to help someone else out; folks who had worked hard their whole lives, bought their dream home, only to see it taken away from them because they had been hit by some hard times that they could not get out from under in time to save their home.

I made an offer on the home, and they walked away with some money in their pocket, and I had a great investment property. Because of their hard times, the previous owners had neglected some of the maintenance on the home, and weren't able to update anything for some time, so the appliances, layout and other aspects of the home were very dated. Carpets were stained, every room needed painting, and the yard was a wreck. But, most of the work was cosmetic, and easily completed by a do-it-yourself kind of guy like I was at the time.

While I was young in my career, I kept working on my little house. By this time, three years later, I was married, and my wife was pregnant. The little run down house that I had purchased those three years prior was now a sweet little home in a desirable neighborhood. I liked the house, and could have lived there longer, but as you know from the beginning of this book, we got an offer on the house. The offer was significantly more than what I had put into it, so I sold it.

Now, tell me where you can put your money in an account, wait three years, and you have 25% more than what you put into the account?. This happens in real estate all the time. Yes, the market goes up and down. We had a tough downturn in 2006-2009, but, in general, those prices have recovered, and most of the country is experiencing a healthy housing market. So real estate investments are a real opportunity for you to gain personal wealth and financial security.

Through the years, I have added to that original real estate investment by purchasing residential properties, as well as commercial properties. At times, certain properties are also rental properties, so I have an income stream from these investments, and the rent more than covers the expenses related to the properties. I've also purchased vacant land. Through all of this, I've been able to create multiple and independent income streams, completely separate from my daily business activities.

There are lots of ways to get started, and many resources, courses and workshops out there that get into the nitty gritty of true real estate wealth, so I won't go into that type of detail here. Heck, even the McDonald's corporation has this figured out. They are one of the richest companies in the world, not because of how many hamburgers they sell, but because they own massive amounts of real estate; approximately 45% of the land, and 70% of the buildings that their more than 37,000 restaurants are located in.

Now, you and I won't become a McDonald's level of real estate investor, but you can amass a certain amount of real estate, and the corresponding financial wealth that comes with that if you do things right. It's important to start somewhere, and that somewhere may be, literally, in your own backyard.

Another way to build wealth in the real estate business, or any business for that matter, is to have a good exit strategy. What I mean by that is to think of your business as a home. You have it, you fix it up, you live in it, improve on it, make changes, and grow the business so that it's worth something. Now, I love my job, but I don't want to work forever; most of us don't. At some point, you need to hang up your hat and either move onto another chapter in your life, or move into retirement, hopefully an independently wealthy and financially secure type of lifestyle.

This can be done by making sure you have a business that is scalable and saleable. Let's take a look at both of these things, and think about how this can work for you as you build your own real estate business.

To be scalable, your real estate business should be able to grow and function without you. What I mean by that is that you have developed systems on how things operate, and they are not dependent on you showing up. If you own a company, and are self-employed, you still work for someone. You. You are your own boss, but it also means that you're still basically an employee. When you build a scalable business, it's different.

A scalable business means that you don't have to show up every day. You might check in once in a while, show up for quarterly business retreats or meetings, but the business is running on its own because you have set up the systems for that to happen. You receive income from that business, and you can focus on something else in the real estate field, or something completely different. This also sets up your business to be saleable.

A saleable business is one that is attractive to investors. Someone who wants what you have created. In other words, your exit strategy, and even your retirement strategy, might be to scale your business, and set it up so that it is an attractive purchase for someone else to buy from you. Let's say, for example, that you have a successful real estate brokerage firm in southern Florida. You have several offices throughout your county, your brokerage firm enjoys a solid reputation and is well-known in the community.

One of your competitors might be very interested in acquiring your brokerage firm, so that they can expand their operations overnight. If you've successfully scaled your firm, where a new owner can take over operations easily, you can make millions more than you ever could by selling other people's houses.

So, I guess what I'm saying here is that if you want to make big money in real estate, you have to think big. You have to think beyond, perhaps, what you considered when you first decided to become a real estate agent. How far do you want to go? How far can you go? Set your sites on the long-term, and see what you can do to expand your earning and wealth potential.

Some brokerages may offer you the opportunity to build a business within a business, and to participate in retirement benefits later on. If this is something that interests you, be sure to ask brokers as you are interviewing.

THE "RETIREMENT" EXERCISE

You may be just starting out, but let's jump forward and take a look at what retirement may look like for you:

What date would you like to retire	
How much annual income will you need to retire?	
How much net worth will you need to generate that income?	
What is your current net worth?	
What is the gap between current and future net worth?	
How will you fill that gap?	

Chapter 14

Have Fun!

So, here we are at the end of the book. I hope that you have found some of the ideas in this book helpful, and that it has given you some solid ideas about how you can get started in real estate, build your clientele and referral list, and, eventually, get out of the real estate business in a way that guarantees you financial independence and wealth.

Looking back to 1987 when I first got my real estate license, I can't believe where I started and where I am now. If you had asked me then what my career would look like now, I would have had no idea. Today I can tell you that through the world of real estate, I have met thousands of people, made hundreds of friends, and been blessed with running a fantastic company with 150 of the best employees on planet earth. I've had financial success which has allowed me to travel, to invest in other areas, and to pursue hobbies and activities that I may not have otherwise been able to engage in.

My wife and I have raised two beautiful daughters in a standard of living significantly higher than when I was a kid. I've been able to donate money to help others in a way that I want to help, and I've been able to be involved with charities and spend my time doing things I want to do. I never could have imagined doing this years ago.

But, for me, the most important thing through the years is that I've had fun. A lot of fun. Fun meeting people, fun doing deals, fun in training, learning, and educating myself, fun in teaching classes and seeing thousands of people striving to meet their goals and dreams.

I've had fun building a business, steering around potholes and pitfalls, and fun planning the future. It's been fun building an award-winning company that has been rated by its employees as one of the best places to work in South Florida for the past 5 years.

And now I have fun looking back on what we've done and helping you decide where you are going. I don't know what your future will look like, but I hope you take these lessons to heart, put some dreams into plans, and plans into action so 30 years from now you can look back and say how much fun you've had doing what you wanted to do.

ABOUT JOHN GREER

Gold Coast Owner

John Greer has had a passion for educating adults for many years. Licensed in real estate since 1987, John began his career in professional education by tutoring students with learning disabilities who had a hard time passing the Florida real estate license exam. John then moved to classroom education where he taught tens of thousands of students. John has been the co-owner and Director of Gold Coast Schools since 1994. During this time, he has worked with hundreds of instructors to help improve their instructional techniques, student retention, and student pass rates. John has also written and developed many real estate textbooks and online courses, as well as one of the first instructor continuing education programs to be approved by the state of Florida.

John's educational background started with a Bachelor's degree in Business which he earned at night while enlisted in the United States Air Force. John later completed a Master's degree in Adult Education and a Doctorate in Educational Leadership and Management. John's doctoral research involved improving the professional development of instructors through the creation of feedback loops and coaching.

In addition to local trade organizations and Associations of Realtors, John has been very involved with the local community. He served on the board of the local Leukemia and Lymphoma Society for six years including one year as Treasurer, and two years as President. John served as Board Chair for the College of Education Advisory Board of Florida Atlantic University, and served on the FAU Foundation Advisory Board. He has also served on numerous Florida Real Estate Commission task forces, including syllabus development for both the Sales Associate and Broker courses, and on the Florida Panthers Blueprint Advisory Board. John is also a member of Vistage and a participant in Strategic Coach.

Gold Coast Professional Schools, LLC, is Florida's leading provider of licensure education training in the fields of Real Estate, Construction, Insurance, CAM, Mortgage Loan Origination, Appraisal, and Property Management. In 2016, Gold Coast acquired Bert Rodgers Schools of Real Estate. Gold Coast has placed in the top 10 of the Sun Sentinel's Top South Florida Workplaces every year since 2015, and was ranked the number one medium-sized business to work for in south Florida in 2019.

John resides in Delray Beach Florida with his wife Jacqueline. While not working John plays ice hockey, coaches high school hockey at Marjory Stoneman Douglas High School, and enjoys many outdoor activities including offshore fishing, scuba diving, and camping.

FINAL ASSIGNMENT

Now it's time to put it all together. If you've been doing the assignments at the end of each chapter, you should now have the basics for your business plan. If you have not done the exercises, take the time to complete them now and package them together as your business plan:

1 Why?
2 Become and Expert
3 Choosing the right broker
4 Interviewing
5 Training Plan
6 Prospecting
7 Branding
8 Relationship Builder
9 Budget
10 Time Tracker/Delegation identifier
11 Education Plan
12 Income Expansion
13 Retirement planner
14 Putting it all together

Thank You

Thank you to all of the people that have played a role in my life, and thus a role in this book. Of course, it all started with my parents. Thanks Mom and Dad for instilling the moral compass and drive to succeed that have led me on this journey.

Next, I want to thank my wife Jacqueline, and daughters Kaitlin and Sydney. You've put up with a lot of my crazy ideas over the years. Though I've tried to spend as much family time as possible, we've always had to balance family and work time.

Thank you to all of the Gold Coast team members that I've had the pleasure of working with over the years. Your dedication to our student's success is un-paralleled in the industry.

Thank you to all the amazing students who have trusted Gold Coast with their education over the past 50 years. We have some incredible success stories, and even a few marriages, from people who started their careers with us.

Finally, thank you to all of the friends, mentors, and industry professionals that I've been able to learn from over the years.

John Greer

Made in the USA
Columbia, SC
04 June 2020